Lockheed C-130 Hercules
and Its Variants

second edition revised and expanded

Lockheed C-130

HERCULES

and Its Variants

second edition revised and expanded

CHRIS REED

Schiffer Military History
Atglen, PA

Dedication

To all the men and women who have flown, maintained,
and sometimes given their lives in C-130s over the decades.

Thanks must be given to all the persons who contributed photos, memories, and other material for this book; without your aid this work would not have been possible.

List of Photo Contributors:
Doug Oliver/Lockheed Martin
Nick Challoner
Paul Hart
Anders Edback
Sherman R. Pyle
Edwards AFB History Office/Raymond Puffer
Neil Dunridge
Peter E. Davies
Robert M. Robinson
911th Airlift Wing, USAF Reserve
Sig Grudzinski/ERSE
Takanobu Okamura
Dr. James Moore/T.B.M. Aviation
John M. Sepp/PIMA Air Museum

Other Assistance:
Phil Rowe
Bruce M. Bailey

Other Schiffer Books by the Author:
Lockheed C-5 Galaxy, ISBN: 978-0-7643-1205-2

Other Schiffer Books on Related Subjects:
The Age of Orion: The Lockheed P-3, David Reade,
ISBN: 978-0-7643-0478-1
The "C" Planes: U.S. Cargo Aircraft from 1925 to the Present, Bill Holder & Scott Vadnais, ISBN: 978-0-88740-912-7

Copyright © 2017 by Chris Reed

Library of Congress Control Number: 2017930356

Cover design by Molly Shields
Type set in ArTarumianKamar/Times LT Std

ISBN: 978-0-7643-5333-8
Printed in China

Published by Schiffer Publishing, Ltd.
4880 Lower Valley Road
Atglen, PA 19310
Phone: (610) 593-1777; Fax: (610) 593-2002
E-mail: Info@schifferbooks.com
Web: www.schifferbooks.com

For our complete selection of fine books on this and related subjects, please visit our website at www.schifferbooks.com. You may also write for a free catalog.

Schiffer Publishing's titles are available at special discounts for bulk purchases for sales promotions or premiums. Special editions, including personalized covers, corporate imprints, and excerpts, can be created in large quantities for special needs. For more information, contact the publisher.

We are always looking for people to write books on new and related subjects. If you have an idea for a book, please contact us at proposals@schifferbooks.com.

Contents

CHAPTER ONE

The Early Years

Introduction

Hercules. Herk. Herky-Bird. Four-Engined Fighter. Whatever its popular name, Lockheed's C-130 remains the world's premier tactical airlifter more than four decades after its first flight. Conceived in the depths of the Cold War, the Hercules has hauled troops, vehicles, cargo, and refugees in several major wars, numerous interventions, and countless relief and humanitarian missions. There have also been a dizzying array of special purpose models, filling such diverse roles as airborne early warning, weather reconnaissance, side-firing gunship, electronic and photographic intelligence, arctic resupply, search and rescue, and aerial refueling tanker.

The genesis of the C-130 program dates back to the 1940s. World War II saw the first extensive use of tactical airlift, and by the end of the war the concept of moving troops into battlefield areas by air had been proven. The USAAF fought the war

Fairchild's C-82 Packet (foreground) and its C-119 successor were early attempts to produce a purpose-designed tactical transport. The C-82 went out of service in 1955, but the final reserve C-119s were not replaced until the 1970s. *Chris Reed*

equipped for the most part with Curtiss C-46 Commandos and Douglas C-47s, and both types proved to be workhorses. But these aircraft were basically adapted airliners, and what was needed was a purpose-designed type able to carry both men and large military items such as vehicles to the front.

During the war, successful use was made of gliders for transporting vehicles and heavy equipment during airborne operations. However, the advantages of a powered aircraft that could land, disgorge its cargo, and take off again under its own power were obvious, and there were several attempts to turn gliders into powered transports; Messerschmitt created the six-engined Me323 Gigant heavy transport from the equally large Me321, and after the war the US experimental XCG-20 assault glider formed the basis for the C-123B Provider. And in the UK, a late version of the General Aircraft Hamilcar heavy glider was fitted with a pair of Mercury engines, and the basic design helped form the starting point for the later Bristol 170.

An early attempt to meet the need for an entirely new tactical transport was Fairchild's F-78, which was designated as the C-82 Packet. This aircraft used a layout not dissimilar to that of the smaller Lockheed P-38 fighter, with a central fuselage and twin engine/tailbooms. The Packet could carry 41 paratroopers, and a clamshell door at the rear of the fuselage allowed for easy loading of equipment and vehicles. Powered by R-2800 engines, the first XC-82 flew in September 1944. However, by the time that the C-82 was ready for service the war had ended, and the planned large-scale production was pared down to a mere 220 aircraft. The C-82 was phased out of USAF service in 1954, and a year later a dozen examples were supplied to the Brazilian Air Force, which used them for paradrop missions for the next twelve years.

Although the C-82 program had been prematurely halted, the basic concept was to be developed further, and in 1947 Fairchild flew the XC-82B, later redesignated the C-119A. The

C-130A 54-1638 of the 95th TAS, USAF Reserve at RAF Greenham Common, 23 July 1983. *Robbie Robinson*

"Dollar Nineteen" or "Flying Boxcar" as it became known had a redesigned flight deck, wider fuselage, and Pratt & Whitney R-4360 Wasp Major engines. The type went into production in 1949, and the line remained open until 1955, after 1,112 aircraft had been built. Although replaced by the C-130 and other types, the C-119 remained in service for a number of years. Indeed, the type was not completely phased out of US second-line use until the early 1970s, when C-130As became available. The last military C-119s were retired by Taiwan in December 1997.

The C-119 first saw combat in Korea and made a name for itself in several airborne operations, including the dropping of heavy bridge sections to the Marines retreating from Chosin following the Chinese entry into the war. However, the C-119 also encountered severe problems, chief among them propellers that tended to disintegrate in flight. The tactical situation in Korea kept the C-119s flying, but for a time they were restricted to cargo missions until the propeller problems could be solved. The C-119G model had new props, but the Dollar Nineteen's problems in Korea had helped seal its fate, and the USAF was soon looking for a new aircraft to equip Tactical Air Command troop carrier squadrons.

Four companies were involved in the search for a C-119 replacement. Fairchild hoped to get the business, as did Boeing (maker of the C-97), Douglas (with extensive experience from the C-47, C-54, and C-124 programs), and finally Lockheed, whose sole large military transport (discounting the limited production Constitution) was the C-121, an adaptation of the Constellation airliner. The basic requirements set down by the USAF were for an aircraft that could carry 25,000 lbs of cargo for 1,100 miles on combat resupply missions, 92 troops, or 64 paratroops as a troop carrier, or 38,000 lbs as a logistical transport. The aircraft would also have to operate from rough forward airstrips.

Lockheed was seemingly the underdog in the competition, but its Model 82, created by designers at the company's "Skunk Works" division at Burbank, California, was extremely well thought out, with a configuration that would set the standard for airlifters. This had a pressurized cargo hold some nine feet high, ten feet wide, and 41 feet long. Straight in loading was accomplished via a rear two-piece cargo door, the bottom half forming a loading ramp when lowered all the way down. Unlike the C-119, which had to have its rear clamshell doors removed for heavy airdrop missions, the Model 82 could simply lower the ramp, drop the load, and raise the ramp again, sealing the hold. Putting loads into the aircraft was also easier, as this could be done in a "straight in" fashion. Early production

C-130A 74-1640, showing the original "Roman Nose" appearance with the blunt APN-42 radome. *Robbie Robinson*

Overall view of -1640, still wearing the Southeast Asia scheme in June 1979. *Robbie Robinson*

Lockheed's (now Lockheed Martin's) Marietta facility continues to build Herks some four and a half decades after the first YC-130 flight. Seemingly unspectacular when first created, the C-130 will outlive the later turbofan-powered C-141B Starlifter, which itself started out as an evolution of the never-built GL-207 Super Hercules. *LMASC*

aircraft would have a 6*7.4 foot cargo door on the port side of the forward fuselage, but this was deleted on later models. Paratroop doors were fitted to the fuselage aft of the landing gear fairings, with airstream deflectors that could be raised to allow a clean separation from the aircraft. The two-spar wing used machined skin panels to cut down on riveting, and contained four integral fuel tanks, with each inboard tank holding 1,265 gallons, while the outboards each contained 1,360 gallons.

The high-mounted, high-aspect wing mounted four Allison T56 turboprops, and the Model 82 would be the first US production aircraft to use this type of engine. Using a turbine core fitted with a reduction gear and propeller, the T56 is a constant

Early C-130A with the original three-bladed props. The later four-bladed units were much better for crew comfort, producing less noise. The A-models were hard-worked, flying for the USAF until the early 1990s. *LMASC*

speed powerplant, meaning that the rate of fuel bum increases or decreases the power transmitted to the props.

The spacious cockpit had no fewer than 22 windows covering nearly forty square feet, allowing the flight crew excellent visibility during airdrop missions. Standard flight deck crew would be four, with a navigator and flight engineer supplementing the pilots.

Tandem main landing gear with low-pressure tires for operations from forward fields was fitted in pods faired to the sides of the fuselage. This kept the interior clear of obstructions, while the tandem arrangement meant that for operations from dirt runways the forward wheel would plow a path for the following unit. The hydraulically actuated nose gear had a range of movement of 60 degrees to either side.

As a point of reference, a rival design by Boeing, the Model 495, had a high-mounted inverted gull wing, and would have been powered by four Pratt & Whitney T34P-6 engines each rated at 5,700 shp. Unlike the Lockheed design, the 495's main landing gear would have been housed in the inboard engine nacelles.

On July 11, 1951, it was announced that the Model 82 would be bought by the USAF, with the military designation C-130 and the popular name of Hercules. The initial order was for a pair of YC-130s, which would be built at the Burbank plant. These would be the only C-130s built in California, as all production aircraft would be constructed at Lockheed's plant at Marietta, Georgia, where B-29s had been assembled by Bell a decade earlier. The facility had later been used by Lockheed to refurbish reactivated Superfortresses, and to build B-47Es under license. It had always been intended that C-130 production would be the responsibility of the Georgia division, and well before the first flight the functional mockup (completed

Only the uniforms of the troops and the C-130's camouflage mark this as a relatively recent photograph, as such scenes have been repeated many times worldwide since the late 1950s. *LMASC*

in March 1952) and the engineering staff had been transferred to Marietta.

The first YC-130 (53-3396) flew on August 23, 1954, on a flight from Burbank to the USAF's flight test facility at Edwards AFB, later being joined by its sister ship 53-3397. The precursors 6f a long line, the prototypes themselves were ironically short-lived, being broken up in the 1960s after having been redesignated as NC-130 testbeds.

The first production Hercules was the C-130A, designated as the Model 182 by Lockheed. The very first C-130A, 53-3129, was rolled out of the Marietta plant on March 10, 1955, and flew on April 7. Later nicknamed *First Lady*, -3129's career was almost over as soon as it began, as on her third flight an engine caught fire, forcing an emergency landing. Although the left wing was burned completely off, the crew walked away from the accident, and -3129 would be repaired to fly again, finally retiring as an AC-130A on September 10, 1995.

Whereas the YCs were built with rounded tail tops, the production aircraft had flat-topped tails with an anticollision beacon on top. Other differences included 450-gallon external tanks and T56A-1A engines each rated at 3,750 shp. There were the usual teething problems; the original Curtiss-Wright propellers with electric pitch control were troublesome, and had to be replaced by Aero Products props with hydraulic pitch control. Later C-130s had four-bladed Hamilton Standard props, again with hydraulic control; C-130As were refitted with these props, but some flew in the original configuration for years.

Another refit program for early Herks would replace the APS-42 radar with an AN/APN-59 set; this resulted in the original "roman nose" appearance, giving way to the familiar "pinnochio nose" configuration. Some C-130As kept the origi-

nal radar for decades; the basic APN-59 set remains in service into 1997, the last variant being the APN-59F. The -59F can be used in weather, beacon interrogation, mapping, and search modes. Maximum range is quoted at 240 miles, although of course in actual service this figure can be lowered due to a number of factors. Care must be taken when using the radar on the ground, as a radiation hazard area for ground personnel then exists to the front and side of the nose, while beyond this is an area where the radar energy could ignite spilled fuel or explosive material. The APN-59 is becoming increasingly difficult to support, and the set's performance and reliability deficiencies when compared to newer systems mean that many C-130s are likely to be refitted with more modern radars.

Well, before the C-130A entered service, the aircraft was clearly seen as a winner. In mid-1956, an airdrop record was set when a C-130A dropped a platform loaded with thirteen and a half tons of iron ballast. In October of that year the 3245th Test Group undertook a series of operational tests from Pope AFB, North Carolina, in conjunction with Army forces from the 82nd Airborne from nearby Fort Bragg. The combat type missions involved rapid turn arounds and carried all manner of cargo, ranging from rations to trucks and self-propelled guns. During these trials, a C-130 demonstrated its ability to airdrop

Over the years, C-130s have airdropped everything from meals to light artillery. *LMASC*

Although created as a means of supporting conflict, the Hercules has made a career of hauling relief supplies to victims of natural and man-made disasters. *LMASC*

a Marine Ontos recoilless rifle vehicle weighing in at 22,253 lb, as well as its crew. A belly landing was made (not on purpose!) during the tests on October 26, but little damage was done.

The 463rd Troop Carrier Wing of TAC at Ardmore AFB was the first operational C-130 unit, taking delivery of four aircraft on December 9, 1956. These had flown in directly from Marietta, and staged an airdrop before landing at their new base. Within two years of the 463rd taking delivery of its first aircraft, C-130As were flying with units at Sewart AFB, Tennessee, Evreaux AB, France, and Ashiya AB, Japan.

For TAC pilots accustomed to smaller twin-engined transports, the Hercules was a quantum leap forward. Despite the aircraft's size, its hydraulically boosted flight control surfaces with electrically powered trim tabs made for ease of handling. Coupled with the excess turboprop power, it is little wonder that former C-47, C-82, and C-119 crews began referring to the C-130 as a "four-engined fighter." Several generations later, aircrew and ground personnel the world over still attest to the Herk's capabilities.

C-130A production amounted to 231 aircraft; the only export customer for new-build machines being the Royal Australian Air Force, which bought twelve (A97-3205/3216) powered by T56A-11 engines. These have since been retired, with some examples being passed on to Chad. Finally phased out of US service (save for a few examples) by the early 1990s, C-130As are still flying with several smaller air forces and in civilian colors.

Former USAF C-130A in UN colors for participation in World Food program relief flights. *Sherman R. Pyle*

WFP C-130A taxiing past pallets of relief supplies. *Sherman R. Pyle*

Although having started out as one of the first Herks, C-130A -0525 is seen here configured as a pseudo AC-130U with side-mounted cannon and ECM pods, for electronic testing at the USAF Rome Lab's Stockbridge Facility. *Sig Grudzinski/Erse*

A number of C-130As are also operating as commercial firebombers in the western US, flying under contract for the US Forestry Service. These aircraft entered service in the 1980s, replacing older piston-engined aircraft. The firefighting missions demand as much skill as combat flights, and among the casualties include a C-130A (N135FF) of the Helmut Valley Flying Service which exploded in flight over California in August 1994 and impacted a mountain in the Antelope Valley, killing all three crewmembers.

Even in retirement, some C-130As still serve a useful purpose. The USAF's Rome Laboratory uses a number of retired aircraft as static testbeds for measuring the "coverage" of ECM systems and other electronic emitters. C-130A 56-525 is one of these, this particular Herk having entered service in October 1957 and then modified as a C-130A-II *Rivet Victor*, serving with the 7406th Support Squadron and periodically returning to Temco (later to be Raytheon E-Systems) for updating. -0525 later flew as a standard transport with ANG units in California,

Minnesota, and Ohio. It arrived at Griffis AFB in June 1986 for conversion to its final role, subsequently being taken apart for transportation to the lab's Stockbridge, New York, site for reassembly and pedestal mounting. Now part of the "Upside Down Air Force," -0525 has tested antenna configurations for the MC-130H, AC-130U, and other Hercules models.

The C-130A was superseded on the line by the B-model, which first flew on November 20, 1958. The principal difference was the installation of T56-A-7 engines each rated at 4,050 shp. Qualifying the C-130 airframe for the new engines involved fitting the first YC-130 with T56-A-7s on the inboard stations. The -7s were mounted ten inches farther forward than the older models, to improve the center of gravity. The C-130B was also heavier than the A-model, had an all-AC electrical

-0525 makes an inverted flight of sorts as it is lowered for mounting. The aircraft's wings were later reattached. *Sig Grudzinski/Erse*

Another inverted view of -0525. In the background can be seen the facility's B-52G. *Sig Grudzinski/Erse*

Tanker 64, one of the permanently configured air tanker C-130s operated for the US Forestry Service. *Dr. James K. Moore*

system, strengthened horizontal stabilizer, and a fuel dumping system. In the beginning, Lockheed had hoped to sell 100-150 C-130Bs, and ended up building 132, with deliveries ending in March 1963. Like the C-130A, the B-model is now out of US service, but ex-USAF machines have in recent years been transferred to air forces all over the world.

In years past, mention was often made of the fact that of the few major air forces not to use the Hercules, the majority were in the Soviet sphere of influence. This was certainly true at the time, but the collapse of the USSR has led to new defense alliances being forged, and the Hercules has begun to appear on the other side of the dismantled Iron Curtain, as former Warsaw Pact members start to re-equip with Western aircraft. The first to do so was Romania, which took delivery of a pair of C-130Bs from USAF stocks on October 25, 1996. A further two were turned over in December of that year.

South Africa bought seven C-130Bs in the early 1960s, before the beginning of the UN arms embargo on that country, and the type is still in service some three decades later. In 1996, with apartheid and the embargo now in the past, the B-models were supplemented by ex-USN C-130Fs and former USAF C-130Bs. The South African Herks are to remain active into the 21st Century, and in 1997 the first example arrived in England to be rebuilt with a glass cockpit by Marshalls of Cambridge.

Whereas the C-130A/B models were bought primarily for tactical transport of troops and logistical support of TAC combat wings, the next Hercules variant would take on a new role, that of limited strategic airlifter. By the early 1960s, the Military Air Transport Service (from 1968 Military Airlift Command - MAC) was faced with a large fleet of slow and outmoded propeller-driven transports that could not meet the command's need for fast intercontinental airlift. To remedy this,

Tanker 63 taxiing. *Dr. James K. Moore*

The C-130 air tankers wear civilian colors and high visibility bands and numbers. *Dr. James K. Moore*

C-130B 57-0526 making a rocket assisted take off. This aircraft subsequently became a JC-130B. *USAF via Edwards AFB History Office*

South African C-130B 401 landing at RAF Fairford on 17 July 1996. Now better than three decades old, the SAAF B-models are being refitted with glass cockpits for continued service. *Neil Dunridge*

The SAAF applied special markings on 401 to celebrate the service's 75th anniversary. Unit is 28 Squadron. *Robbie Robinson*

turbofan-powered C-135Bs and C-141As were ordered, but MATS also turned to the Hercules. The C-130E could carry an additional 2,720 gallons of fuel in large external tanks outboard of the engines, giving the Herk sufficient range to reach what was then West Germany nonstop, a critical capability for NATO missions. Even the vast Pacific could be crossed with a single stop in Hawaii, which would prove vital during the Vietnam years. Also, the aircraft's maximum payload capacity was increased to 45,000 lbs. The C-130E retained the B-model's T56-A-7 engines, but many of the special derivatives of the basic type have been reengined with T56-A-15s.

The first C-130E flew on August 25, 1961, and a total of 389 examples were produced for MATS and TAC, with production reaching 488 for all users. As most C-130Hs have gone

Now older than some of their crewmen, the C-130Es started life in the pre-camouflage days of the early 1960s. *LMASC*

As most C-130Hs have gone to the USAF Reserve and Air National Guard, the older C-130Es have remained in frontline USAF service. Aircraft 64-0502 of the 86th Wing is seen here at Mildenhall on 29 May 1995. *Neil Dunridge*

Royal Saudi Arabian Air Force C-130E at Manchester, England. *Sherman Pyle*

to reserve and guard units, the C-130E has remained in frontline service into the late 1990s.

MATS also incorporated several Navy Air Transport Squadrons, and these also received C-130s. Navy MATS units included VR-7, which converted from the R7V/C-121, VR-8, another former Constellation unit, and VR-22, which had formerly flown the R6D/C-118. The Navy squadrons were removed from the MATS mission when the service became the Military Airlift Command in 1968.

Only eight E-models were built with provisions for the forward cargo door, and earlier aircraft had theirs sealed after a C-130B lost its door in flight. This incident took place on March 3, 1964, during a flight over the Great Smokey Mountains of Tennessee. One crewman was sucked out, with another holding on to a tiedown cable until he could be pulled back in. Major damage was done to the port side of the fuselage, and debris hit an engine, knocking it out. The pilot, a RAF exchange officer, managed to bring the stricken Hercules in to an emergency landing at McGhee-Tyson AFB, although hydraulic damage had also been incurred, and the nosegear would not lower.

The frequent need to conduct airdrops in all weather conditions and into areas without any navigational aids led to approximately 50 C-130Es being fitted with the Adverse Weather Aerial Delivery System (AWADS) radars (dual X and Ka-band) for service as pathfinders. Aircraft fitted with Station Keeping

C-130E 62-1822 at Reno, Nevada on 14 October 1995. Despite wearing the "HW" tailcode of Howard AFB, Panama this aircraft may have been on the strength of the Nevada Air National Guard. *Neil Dunridge*

C-130E 63-9815 of the 314th TAW in a desert camo scheme during a visit to RAF Alconbury in August 1981. *Robbie Robinson*

C-130E 69-6582 of the 435th TAW in a brown/tan scheme, with small national insignia, at RAF Alconbury in April 1982. *Robbie Robinson*

Equipment can fly in formation with AWADS-equipped transports and achieve precision airdrops by receiving cues from the pathfinders.

Early Crises

In the summer of 1958, the Hercules had only been in service for a short while, and the conflict in Southeast Asia was still some years off. However, the first of what would be many international crises in the Herk's career loomed large in the Middle East. On July 14, a coup in Iraq toppled the government there and shattered the Arab Federation union between Iraq and Jordan that had only been in place since the previous February. Other Arab governments feared that they could be next, and President Chamoun of Lebanon requested US aid to stabilize his country. The first response to this was the landing of Marines at Beirut, but USAFE C-130s were also used to bring in

Army Airborne forces. The transports also supported TAC aircraft in Turkey, and stood ready to assist the British forces in Jordan. Fortunately, both the US and UK operations did not meet with opposition, and the interventions served to stabilize the region.

In August 1958, shortly after the height of the crisis in the Middle East, an even more dangerous problem arose on the other side of the globe. Since the 1949 victory of the Communist Chinese on the mainland, Nationalist forces on Formosa (Taiwan) had occupied the islands of Quemoy, off the port of Xiamen (Amoy) and to the north, Matsu near Fuzhou (Foochow). Chiang Kai Shek's Nationalist forces used these islands as foward bases for operations against the mainland, and there were frequent skirmishes throughout the 1950s. Tensions were reaching the boiling point by 1958 over the continued reinforcement of the islands, and the planned US deploy-

C-130E 64-0504 of the 317th TAW in an experimental gray paint scheme at RAF Mildenhall, Suffolk on June 11, 1980. *Robbie Robinson*

C-130E 64-681 served as the personal aircraft of the commander of the 86th Airlift Wing in 1996. *Robbie Robinson*

ment of Matador SSMs to Formosa itself. In August, the Communists began vicious artillery attacks against the islands, pouring in tens of thousands of shells daily. President Eisenhower ordered USAF units to Formosa to provide cover for the supply convoys to the islands and the US ground troops on Formosa itself. Aside from supporting US Army and Nationalist units on the islands, C-130s also brought in supplies and munitions for the deployed tactical aircraft, which included F-104s, F-100s, RF-101s, and KB-50J tankers. In the air, Chinese MiGs were active as well, and clashes with Nationalist F-86s took place. It has long been rumored that the USAF's F-104s also scored some MiG kills, but this has never been confirmed, and as far as is known, no C-130s were subjected to aerial attack during this period.

C-130s were heavily involved in the Dominican Republic Crisis of 1965, which followed several years of instability in the carribbean nation. Fearful that Communist elements would come to power following the latest in a series of revolts, President Johnson ordered in a Marine force on April 28, and elements of the 82nd Airborne Division were lifted to forward locations by C-130s and C-124 Globemasters; the Army forces were subsequently airlanded at San Isidro Airbase, from where they linked up with the Marines, serving to keep rival Dominican forces apart and keep the peace. American transport aircraft also provided logistical support for the Organization of American States forces that gradually replaced US troops.

Vietnam

Although the Hercules has been involved in combat operations worldwide, it was the US involvement in Southeast Asia from 1960 to 1975 that helped cement the type's reputation. Well before large-scale overt American military intervention began, C-130 squadrons of the 315th Air Division from bases at Tachikawa, Japan, and Naha, Okinawa, were engaged in bring-

ing supplies to the US-backed forces in the Laotian civil war. The US and USSR later brought about a truce, and the Laotian flashpoint cooled for a time, but the whole southeast asian region was about to come to a boil.

The first US advisors to the South Vietnamese armed forces began arriving in 1961, and after the Gulf of Tonkin incident in August 1964 C-130s were tasked with supporting the ever-increasing buildup of both ground forces and tactical aircraft in South Vietnam. While continuing to be based on Okinawa, the 315th set up a forward location at Tan Son Nhut Airbase near Saigon, and was soon flying missions into every area of South Vietnam. While not able to operate from some of the extremely marginal fields used by Army CV-2 Caribou and USAF C-123 Providers, the Hercules could carry far more payload than the smaller piston-engined transports, and could do so at higher speeds. In a war of mobility, the capabilities of the Hercules were pivotal in quickly moving men and material through a country-wide war zone.

In 1965, the growing need for airlift led to the deployment of the 314th Troop Carrier Wing, equipped with C-130Es, and the 463rd, flying B-models. Later, the 6315th Operations Group, which flew missions with C-130As would be redesignated as the 374th TCW. In October of the next year, the 834th Air Division gained control of C-130s when they were operating in Vietnam. Unlike the smaller transports, C-130s were not permanently based in Vietnam, but the units involved maintained forward deployments from their home bases on Okinawa and Taiwan. Like other USAF aircraft of the early 1960s, the C-130s were uncamoflaged when the conflict in Southeast Asia began, but the prewar finish soon gave way to a tricolor camo pattern.

Attempting to destroy the Central Office for South Vietnam (COSVN), the VC headquarters unit that straddled the

C-130E 64-0539 of the 41st Airlift Squadron was attached to the 23rd Composite Wing, the descendant of the 23rd Fighter Group and the American Volunteer Group (AVG) "Flying Tigers" of World War II. *Robbie Robinson*

64-496 of the 2nd Airlift Squadron was another aircraft of the 23rd Composite Wing, seen here at Alconbury, Cambridgeshire on June 5, 1994. *Robbie Robinson*

South Vietnamese/Cambodian "Fishhook", border region, the US Army launched *Operation Junction City* in February 1967. Part of this operation was the first large scale airborne combat drop (*Junction City Alternate*) since Korea, with C-130s dropping paratroopers from the 173rd Airborne Brigade north of Tay Ninh City on February 22. A total of 13 C-130s dropped nearly 800 combat troops, while another eight aircraft dropped supporting equipment. Junction City lasted into May, but the COSVN managed to survive by retreating into Cambodia. Although other airborne operations would be conducted during the war, *Junction City Alternate* would be the only exercise of such size, as most airmobile missions centered around the use of helicopters.

In November 1967, C-130s were involved in supporting the battles around the Special Forces camp at Dak To. Seeking to draw US forces away from the cities of South Vietnam, the NVA offensive was met by the 173rd, brought in by C-130, as well as elements of the 4th Infantry Division and ARVN units. Two C-130Es were lost on the Dak To airstrip, but US forces proved that they could be rapidly shifted to outlaying areas and back again.

Enemy fire during missions was not the only threat to C-130s in Southeast Asia. In a war with no defined front lines, all areas were subject to attack, particularly airfields. Major VC attacks were common, even at large bases such as Tan Son Nhut, and many US aircraft were the victims of mortars, rock-

C-130E 64-539 of the 23rd, with the sharkmouth and FT tailcode. *Nick Challoner*

C-130E 63-778. *Nick Challoner*

C-130E 63-7818 of the West Virginia ANG. *Courtesy Paul Hart Collection*

ets, recoilless rifle fire, and sapper attacks. Further out in the field, USAF crews unloading C-130s and other transports had to endure the same threats as the Army and Marine troops they were supporting, as did airlift control teams coordinating transport flights in and out of combat zones.

By early 1968, C-130 crews had been involved in the SEA fighting for several years, but one of the most important campaigns was yet to come. A pivotal year in the war, 1968 saw the North Vietnamese launch the Tet Offensive in the south, which was widely perceived by the US media as a defeat of US and ARVN forces, but really marked the beginning of the end of the VC as a major fighting force. However, while the communist insurgents were being fought in the cities of South Vietnam, a major offensive by the North Vietnamese Army was

also ongoing, centered on the Marine combat base at Khe Sanh, near the Laotian border. Ideally placed for interdiction efforts for communist supplies coming through Laos, Khe Sanh was the target of General Vo Nguyen Giap's effort to replicate his victory over the French in 1954, when he besieged and eventually overran the bastion at Dien Bien Phu.

The base had been in existence since 1962, when it served as a camp for Army Green Berets. In early 1967 Marine forces took over the base, and a small 1,500-foot runway was built. This pierced-steel plank facility was useable by C-7A Caribou light transports, but was not long or strong enough for routine Hercules operations. C-130s air delivered supplies for extending the runway with aluminum matting, creating a field that would be invaluable a year later.

C-130E 2465 of the Brazilian Air Force, seen here at RAF Fairford on 17 July 1996. *Neil Dunridge*

C-130E 01468 of the Turkish Air Force's 222 *Filo. Neil Dunridge*

Khe Sanh, like Dien Bien Phu, was the subject of a siege that isolated the base from overland reinforcement and supply, and eventually two NVA divisions were in place around the base. This outnumbered the defenders, which included elements from three Marine regiments and a single ARVN battalion. However, the US had several advantages that the French did not a decade and a half earlier. These included a large transport force, the centerpiece of which was the C-130, and a formidable array of strike aircraft and heavy bombers to hit the encircling NVA. In contrast, the French had had to rely on C-47s and C-119s for resupply, and a small force of B-26s and PB4Y-2s to strike at the Viet Minh. The Marines themselves were far from helpless, with nearly fifty artillery pieces, including huge 175 mm guns.

In early February, a C-130E was hit on the ground at Khe Sanh while bringing in a load of ammunition, but the blaze was put out before the transport could be lost. Less fortunate was KC-130F 149813 which was on a mission to Khe Sanh on February 10. Laden with a cargo of fuel, the aircraft was hit on landing and was enveloped in flames as it rolled out. Seven died in the crash and fire, but the pilot, Chief Warrant Officer Henry Wildfang, and several of his crewmembers managed to get clear of the blazing wreckage.

The remains of Wildfang's tanker did not have a chance to cool before another C-130 was hit and set ablaze the next day. Although two men were lost and the aircraft heavily damaged, the aircraft was not a complete write-off, and over the following days repair crews braved sniper and mortar fire in an effort to get the transport airworthy enough to get out of Khe Sanh. Considering that the "mortar magnets" were vulnerable enough in the air or while doing running offloading on the ground, it was a miracle that the stricken C-130 survived long enough to get back to Da Nang.

The loss of the Marine tanker and the crippling of pair of Air Force C-130s represented a major problem to those run-

ning the airlift. It was agreed that not even the critical conditions at Khe Sanh merited the loss of additional C-130s, which besides being expensive were also needed for other Southeast Asia missions, as well as for the global operations that the USAF was tasked with. Landings by C-130s were stopped, but the airlift requirements of the Marines could not be met without Hercules support, as the smaller C-7s, C-123s, and helicopters could not begin to carry the loads possible with C-130s. Thus, Air Force Hercules crews would continue to make the hazardous flight to Khe Sanh, although they would be spared having to spend time on the ground there.

Faced with such a concentration of enemy firepower, crews had to use a variety of airdrop methods to deliver their supplies into Khe Sanh. Container air drops were one solution, and these could be directed by the Marine radar at the base. However, this had the disadvantage of forcing Marines to recover the supplies from the drop zone, which was outside of the main base. This was quite hazardous, considering that the forward NVA elements had situated themselves very near the US lines in an effort to escape air strikes. Container drops

Dorsal fuselage antenna for Station Keeping Avionics. *Chris Reed*

could consist of up to twelve 1,100 lb loads dropped with the aircraft in a climb, with each load having two 24-foot parachutes. Low Altitude Parachute Delivery System deliveries began on February 16, and these could put supplies right on the runway. LAPES missions entailed a C-130 making a very low pass (3-5 feet) over a runway with the cargo door open; a reefed chute attached to the cargo pallet would then open, pulling the pallet from the aircraft, the load then skidding to a halt on the runway. This did, however, tend to tear up sections of the 3,900 foot aluminum mat runway, and several men were killed on the ground by LAPES accidents. Later in the siege, the Ground Proximity Extraction System (GPES) was revived for deliveries into Khe Sanh. This system used a hook attached to the cargo load; when a low pass was made over the runway the hook engaged an arresting wire, which then pulled the cargo out of the aircraft. Although requiring the ground equipment, GPES was more controllable, and did less damage to the runway.

Thanks to USAF and Marine fixed-wing transports and helicopters, and overwhelming air support, Giap's forces were unable to give their leader the repeat of Dien Bien Phu that he so desired, and the siege of Khe Sanh was broken in April by *Operation Pegasus*, after the base had been encircled for 77 days. On April 13, not long after the siege had been lifted, C-130B 61-0967 was lost in a crash at the base.

Following the end of *Operation Pegasus, Operation Delaware/Lam Son 216* was launched against the North Vietnamese-held A Shau Valley in western South Vietnam. In enemy hands for over two years, A Shau was heavily fortified and protected by numerous antiaircraft emplacements. Supporting the forces of the US 1st Calvalry Division and other airmo-

bile units in the valley was the task of the C-130s, which conducted supply airdrops at A Luoi, one of three abandoned airfields in the area. The predicted good weather never materialized, and the airlift crews had to make instrument approaches into the narrow valley, relying on radar, skill, and luck not to collide with one of the cloud-shrouded mountains. Breaking out of the low ceilings, the aircraft then had to run the gauntlet of intense antiaircraft fire. On April 26, a C-130 was lost in an attempted forced landing at A Luoi after it was raked with enemy fire. A Luoi was also a LZ for helicopter operations, and Army CH-54 Tarhes brought in heavy equipment for combat engineers to rebuild the dirt runway for the fixed-wing transports. By May 3, the runway was restored sufficiently for C-130 operations; two days earlier it had been opened for C-7s. *Operation Delaware* began winding down a week later, and was ended on May 17th.

In May 1968, the Special Forces camp at Kham Duc came under siege. Reinforcements and 105 mm howitzers had been airlifted, landing at the base's 6,000-foot runway, but the enemy had possession of the high terrain, and were able to make the situation untenable for the defenders. An evacuation was ordered on May 12, and the air operation went into reverse, with C-130s pulling out the ground forces under murderous fire. A C-130B was destroyed on takeoff with all aboard, and a C-130A was abandoned after its throttle controls were destroyed in a crash landing. Another C-130A managed to escape the camp after losing one main tire and incurring other damage; the crew won the McKay Trophy for outstanding airmanship on this mission.

Astonishingly, after the camp had been abandoned, a three-man airlift control team led by C-130 pilot Major Jack Gallagher

C-130D 57-0493 at RAF Greenham Common on 24 June 1979. The aircraft by this point was serving with the New York Air National Guard's 139th Tactical Airlift Squadron. *Robbie Robinson*

C-130D 57-0490, distinguishable from later LC-130Hs by virtue of its small C-130A style wing tanks. *Courtesy Paul Hart Collection*

By 1994, the 139th had been redesignated as an airlift squadron, and re-equipped with LC-130Hs such as 83-0490. *Robbie Robinson*

was ordered back in by error, the team having just arrived at Cam Ranh Bay aboard the damaged C-130A. Alone in the now deserted camp, the men were forced to engage the approaching North Vietnamese with small arms while a frantic effort was launched to bring them back out again. One C-123 landed and the team could not reach it, but a second Provider piloted by Lt. Colonel Joe Jackson managed to pick them up. Jackson was awarded the Medal of Honor for this rescue flight.

The Hercules also played an active combatant role in the Vietnam fighting, quite apart from the use of AC-130 gunships. Starting in 1969, C-130Bs of the 463rd were tasked with *Commando Vault* missions, these being strikes with M-121 10,000 lb bombs. Dropped out of the cargo bays, the M-121s dated

back to the 1950s, and had been created for use by the B-36 Peacemaker. These proved ideal for blasting helicopter landing zones, and were also dropped on enemy troop and supply concentrations. A high degree of accuracy was possible, as crews made use of the MSQ-77 *Combat Skyspot* navigational/bombing system, created as a training system for SAC aircrews, and deployed to Asia to guide B-52 strikes. The M-121s were later replaced by new 15,000 lb BLU-82/B weapons. Informally known as the "Daisy Cutter," the BLU-82/B contains just over six and a quarter tons of a mixture of aluminum powder and ammonium nitrate. Upon release this volatile combination forms a cloud over the ground which is then detonated, producing overpressures of over 1,200 psi. Decades after its

Some LC-130Hs have retained the C-130D type high visibility Arctic markings. *Courtesy Paul Hart Collection*

LC-130H -0490 *Pride of Clifton Park*, showing the crew entrance hatch and a side view of the nose ski. *Courtesy Paul Hart Collection*

introduction, the -82 is still regarded as the most powerful conventional bomb in existence. This is apparently not the only time that C-130s have been used as bombers; during its 1965 war with India, Pakistan is reported to have used its Herks to drop conventional iron bombs from opened cargo ramps. Argentina attempted to bomb a British supply ship with a C-130 during the 1983 Falklands War, unsuccessfully.

Less well known than the *Commando Vault* missions was *Operation Carolina Moon*, an attempt to take out the Thanh Hoa Bridge, 80 miles south of Hanoi in North Vietnam. A major supply artery over the Song Ma River, the bridge had taken hits by an enormous amount of explosives, including hits from Walleye guided bombs, with a corresponding loss of US aircrews, yet it still stood. *Carolina Moon* attempted to down the bridge by dropping mines out the back of a C-130 flying upriver, the current then carrying the weapons to the bridge. Considering the losses experienced by much faster and smaller tactical aircraft over the area, the danger to a lumbering C-130 was obvious, but the target was so critical that the plan was okayed.

The first mission was flown on May 30, 1966, with the C-130E "bomber" ingressing at a very low level before climbing to drop five of the 5,000 lb mines. The crew managed to get their aircraft safely out of North Vietnam, but their weapons failed to drop the bridge. The second attempt the next night was a complete failure; the bridge was still standing and C-130E 64-0511 and its entire crew had been lost to North Vietnamese defenses. The bridge stood until March 13, 1972, when it was dropped by USAF F-4s armed with laser-guided Paveway bombs.

Starting in the spring of 1965, C-130As flew *Blind Bat* flareship missions over the Ho Chi Minh Trail system to illuminate targets for strike aircraft. Flying over Laos and even into North Vietnam, the Blind Bats spotted enemy traffic with night goggles and then dropped flares from the opened cargo

bay, essentially serving as the world's largest FACS. C-130A 56-0533 was lost on a *Blind Bat* mission on November 24, 1969, when it was hit by AAA over Laos. Aircraft in the vicinity did not see any of the crew get out before the aircraft exploded, and no signals were received from survival radios. A US-Laotian team excavated the crash site nearly a quarter-century later in October-November 1993 and recovered eight sets of remains, which were subsequently identified.

There was also an attempt to create a more refined illumination model, using high-powered searchlights rather than flares. The RC-130S Battlefield Illumination Airborne System (BIAS) used a pair of C-130As (including 56-0493) fitted with large searchlight pods on both sides of the forward fuselage. These aircraft had the specialized mission equipment removed, and later saw service again as standard transports.

The effort to stop enemy truck traffic on the trail system was a huge one, and naturally the US attempted to find technological solutions to the problem of finding and attacking enemy supply vehicles. Some of these were quite ingenious, while others bordered on the fanciful. One such program, *Commando Scarf*, entailed the dropping of massive quantities of small "button" mines from C-130s, whose explosions would hopefully give away the position of enemy units, as well as slow the work of repair teams that attempted to maintain the trails.

There were other unusual combat uses for the Hercules, such as the deployment of three WC-130As to try and make trails impassable stretches of mud by seeding clouds to make rain. And although deforestation with herbicidal chemicals was the role of the UC-123 *Ranch Hand* aircraft, C-130s did fly missions to drop barrels of contaminated avgas to burn out forests and the concealed VC positions therein.

In 1972, the organization and composition of C-130 units in Southeast Asia was changed. The 314th, based at Chin Chang Kang Airbase in Taiwan was redesignated as the 374th, while the 463rd and the former 374th were brought back to the US With the transfer of C-130A/Bs to reserve forces, the C-130E was the only standard transport model left in the theater.

During this period, the process of "Vietnamization" was underway, with US forces training their South Vietnamese counterparts in the use of modem equipment, and then handing this equipment over to the ARVN and SVNAF. These transfers included ex-USAF C-130As, which gave the SVNAF much needed extra capability; prior to this, the largest transports availible to the service were C-119s and C-123s. Like all South Vietnamese types, the C-130As received new national insignia, which was actually the US "stars and bars" outlined in red.

In the spring of 1972, C-130 crews would face yet another major test in Vietnam, as 125,000 North Vietnamese troops launched offensives across the DMZ and from Cambodia. In the path of the southern offensive was An Loc, 75 miles north of Saigon, which the NVA planned to seize and use as the capitol of a puppet government. Like Khe Sanh four years earlier, An Loc was soon surrounded and cut off from ground resupply and reinforcement. Again, an aerial lifeline was put into place, only this time there were new dangers, including the threat of SA-7 Strela shoulder-fired SAMs. Attempts at dropping supplies from low levels led to the loss of three aircraft, as such missions were well in the envelope of the NVA's conventional antiaircraft artillery, ranging from 23 mm and 57 mm pieces to ZSU-57/2 AA tanks. The solution was to move the C-130s up to higher altitudes, where they made high-speed, radar-assisted airdrops. Later, C-130Es equipped with the Adverse Weather Airdrop System were deployed from the US to participate, along with *Combat Talon* aircraft from Kadena.

In similiar straights to An Loc was Kontum, in central South Vietnam. Airdrops had to be run there also, as the communists had managed to take part of the airfield. Despite the increased risk to aircraft, US airpower managed to stem the tide of the Easter Invasion, and by summer the sieges at An Loc and Kontum had been broken, in the former case after 95 days.

In the fall of 1972, the *Linebacker* and *Linebacker II* air offensives against North Vietnam led at last to the signing of peace accords in Paris, and the subsequent end of US combat involvement in Vietnam. As part of *Operation Homecoming*, the repatriation of US POWs in March 1973, C-130s were flown to Gia Lam Airport north of Hanoi to install navaids, and their crews helped the former captives walk to waiting C-141As for the trip to Clark AB, Phillipines, and from there back to the US. These upbeat missions should have been the Herk's finale in the region, but there was still action to be had in Southeast Asia. Flights continued to be made to Hanoi as part of the peace agreements; on one such mission a pyrotechnic device in the gear of one of the North Vietnamese passengers accidentally went off, filling the aircraft with smoke. The aircraft was landed safely, but this incident did little to further US-North Vietnamese relations.

In the spring of 1975, emboldened by South Vietnam's deteriorating military, and the internal US opposition to getting involved again, the North Vietnamese launched their final offensive, the Ho Chi Minh Campaign, against the south. Without the protection of American air cover, ARVN forces gave way before the NVA, and by late April the North Vietnamese were closing in on Saigon. The SVNAF attempted to slow the advance by using its C-130As as bombers, using BLU-52s transferred from US stores, as well as conventional bombs and napalm. One of these aircraft scored a significant victory by hitting a forward headquarters at Xuan Loc and killing at least 250 (some sources say as many as 1,000) enemy personnel, but these efforts were too little to stop the NVA. Like the rest of the South Vietnamese armed forces, the C-130As were lacking spare parts, and in particular were suffering from fatigue problems.

As the situation continued to deteriorate, a fixed-wing air-lift out of Saigon was begun by the US to bring out the remaining Americans and whatever US dependents and former employees could be accommodated. It was at Tan Son Nhut that the last US Hercules loss of the war took place, when C-130E 72-1297 was hit on the ground during the early morning hours of April 29th. The approach of NVA forces to the outskirts of Saigon ended fixed-wing evacuation flights, but missions by Marine and Air Force H-53 and H-46 helicopters continued for a time, with the helos operating from the US Embassy, which was now surrounded by Vietnamese clamoring to get out of their doomed country. Some South Vietnamese C-130As were abandoned to the communists, but others were flown out as all order broke down, these aircraft flying to Thailand and elsewhere overloaded with refugees. Besides the US and South Vietnamese Herk flights, the Royal Australian Air Force also flew some C-130 missions out of Saigon.

There were other Communist victories in Southeast Asia during 1975. In neighboring Cambodia, the Khymer Rouge ("Red Cambodians") had managed to take control of most of the country, and had encircled the capitol of Pnomh Penh. USAF C-130s began a large-scale airlift to support the city's nearly three million inhabitants, but Congressional opposition to US military operations mandated a switch to civilian-crewed contract flights. The C-130 operation continued, however, as one of the contractors, Bird Air, used C-130s and crews "transferred" from the USAF.

83-0490 on display in the UK, with the JATO bottles attached. The Arctic Herks are the only C-130s to regularly make JATO takeoffs. *Nick Challoner*

Nose ski detail. *Courtesy Paul Hart Collection*

Nose ski detail. *Courtesy Paul Hart Collection*

Despite US efforts, the Pnomh Penh government could not be saved, and the advancing Khymer Rouge troops destroyed a chartered DC-8 with mortar fire on April 8. A helicopter evacuation of remaining US nationals from the enclave, *Operation Eagle Bull*, was initiated on April 12, using CH-53s. Within five days of the American departure, the Khymer Rouge had their final victory, setting the stage for years of genocidal madness. In the 1990s, C-130s would be back in Cambodia, supporting United Nations relief and peacekeeping operations.

The end of US involvement in Southeast Asia coincided with the finale of C-130 operations in Tactical Air Command. The troop carrier/tactical transport mission had been a part of TAC since the command's inception, but in 1975 the C-130s became part of Military Airlift Command. The "tactical" unit designators would be retained, as would the C-130's camouflage, but the TAC tailcodes were removed.

C-130D: First of the Arctic Herks
Prior to the 1950s, the polar regions had little military significance, but this was to change with the beginning of the Cold War. In order to provide warning of a Soviet bomber strike against North America across the arctic, the Distant Early Warning line of radar stations was built across the northern reaches of Canada and the Greenland ice cap, this requiring aerial transport to bring in building materials and equipment, and to later service and supply the finished stations. The impossibility of building conventional runways in many remote arctic regions made it necessary to employ ski-equipped aircraft, which had been used by "bush" pilots for many years. C-123J Providers with skis and wing mounted J44 turbojet booster engines were used, but an aircraft with a larger capacity was needed.

Even before the first C-123J flight, Lockheed had begun testing with three C-130As with skis, with the "Ski 130" flight trials starting on January 29, 1957. Attached to the conven-

tional landing gear, the main ski units were twenty feet long, with the nose unit being half that length; all were five and a half feet wide. Coated on the underside to resist the friction of snow, the skis had a range of travel of eight degrees up and fifteen degrees down to cope with uneven fields. The skis fit almost flush against the underside of the fuselage when not in use. The additional 5,000 lbs of weight did cut into the aircraft's payload and range capacity somewhat, and changing the tires now became a major undertaking.

The three prototypes were later converted back to standard configuration, and Lockheed turned out twelve ski-equipped A-models under the designation C-130D. The initial user unit was the 61st Troop Carrier Squadron at Sewart AFB, Tennessee, but the 17th TCS/TAS "Firebirds" would later receive the C-130Ds. One aircraft, 57-0495, was lost at the DYEIII site in Greenland on July 5, 1972, in a stall-induced crash on takeoff. One civilian was killed, and the aircraft lost its left wing, a portion of the right, and the skis, and incurred other damage. The wreck was stripped and then abandoned. Six others had their skis removed for gravel runway operations in Alaska, and were redesignated as C-130D-6s, although they retained provisions for the ski installation.

Once the construction of the radar sites had been completed, a standard mission for the C-130Ds was the ferrying of fuel to run the generators that powered the radars and other electronics; this was done by fitting fuel tanks from scrappped KC-97s in the cargo holds. The original three-bladed propellers were retained throughout the aircraft's service life; this was done at the expense of crew comfort, as the older props created much more noise inside the aircraft.

The New York Air National Guard's 109th Tactical Airlift Wing took over the mission in 1975, and nine years later the C-130Ds were retired and replaced by four LC-130H2s. Three of the original skibirds are preserved, while at least one was passed on the Peruvian Air Force. The 109th has recently taken

One of the original Marine tankers, KC-130F 149792 of VMGR-352 was still in service on 24 October 1995 when it was seen at El Toro, California. *Neil Dunridge*

on charge three LC-130H3 models, and by 1998 was taking over the Antarctic mission from the Navy.

Tanker/Transports

While the Hercules has not yet appeared with the USAF-style Flying Boom system for refueling aircraft, it has proved well-suited for installation of the British-developed probe and drogue system used by the US Navy, Marines, and many foreign air arms. The first demonstration of this occurred in 1957, when the Marines borrowed a pair of C-130As and fitted them with underwing drogue pods. The successful testing paved the way for procurement of 46 purpose-built GV-1 tankers, which became KC-130Fs when the separate Navy/Marine designation system was abandoned in 1962.

Fitted with a 3,600-gallon fuel tank in the cargo hold and the underwing pods, the KC-130F could, at a radius of 1,000 miles from its home base, transfer 33,000 lbs of fuel to fighters and attack aircraft. Alternatively, both the pods and fuel tank could be quickly taken off and the aircraft used as a standard transport, although the Air Force 463L cargo handling system was not fitted. The C-130F/GV-1U subvariant did not have the refueling gear, and seven examples were bought to equip Navy logistical support squadrons. GV-1/KC-130F deliveries were made between January 1960 and 1962, and the new aircraft gradually replaced the R4Q/C-119, although Marine "Flying Boxcars" would still be in service into the late 1960s.

One KC-130F, BuNo 149798, was loaned to the USN in November 1963 for a unique series of tests intended to demon-

KC-130F 148898 of VMGR-252, seen in April 1980. *Robbie Robinson*

KC-130F 149811 of VMGR-234 at Mildenhall on 11 September 1978. *Robbie Robinson*

strate the type's suitability as a Carrier Onboard Delivery transport. A series of touch and gos (29), unarrested landings (21), and unassisted takeoffs (21) were conducted from the USS *Forrestal* off Jacksonville, Florida, with Lt. James Flatley at the controls of the transport, which had its refueling pods removed for the trials. The largest aircraft ever flown from a carrier, the KC-130F's wingtip cleared the carrier's island by little more than twenty feet. Although successfully tested, the C-130 COD concept was never adopted by the Navy, as the type was far too large for hangar stowage, and would have proved too difficult to integrate into normal operations with a full air wing embarked. A similiar scheme to produce a dedicated COD version of the C-123 Provider also came to naught.

As detailed elsewhere, Marine KC-130Fs were active in Vietnam, principally as tankers for Navy and Marine tactical aircraft, but also as transports, flying with VMGR-152 from its foward base at Da Nang. Aside from the aircraft written off at Khe Sanh, BuNo 149814 was lost in a mid-air collision with a F-4B Phantom on May 18, 1969. KC-130Fs would remain in Marine service into the 1990s, and participated in *Operation Desert Storm*, flying from Bahrain as part of VMGR-252 and -352.

The KC-130F was followed by the KC-130R, a tanker version of the C-130H with two 1,360-gallon tanks between the engines. This variant in turn spawned the KC-130T, which is fitted with the new APS-133 radar and better navaids. A KC-

KC-130Fs were heavily involved in supporting Marine operations during the war in Vietnam, serving as tankers for A-4s, F-8s and Phantoms, as well as flying transport missions. *LMASC*

Navy C-130F transport 149797 of squadron VR-24. *Robbie Robinson*

KC-130F 150689 (Lockheed construction number 3741) of VMGR-152. *Takanobu Okamura*

130T was the 1,800th Hercules to be built, with this aircraft being turned over on December 2, 1986, for service with squadron VMGR-234 of the Marine Reserves. A pair of KC-130T-30s use the C-130H-30 airframe, and were the first stretched Hercules model in US military service. The USMC operates some of the oldest C-130s, and would prefer to replace its earliest tankers with new-build KC-130Js. However, with shrinking budgets and the Corp's need to fund its share of the Joint Strike Fighter program, a stretched-out replacement program looks likely. Some of the older tankers have received avionics updates in the form of secure radios and GPS systems.

While the KC-130s supported Marine fixed-wing types for the first few decades of their service, by the 1980s the Corps began to receive CH-53E Super Stallion heavy lift helicopters that were fitted with refueling probes. This gave Marine forces greatly enhanced strike range, and during the tensions between the Reagan Adminstration and the Sandinista government of Nicaragua, the USMC publicized the fact that with KC-130 support its CH-53Es could reach Central America nonstop from Camp Lejeune, North Carolina, while carrying LAV-25 armored vehicles as sling loads. While this was true, it certainly would have been a grueling mission; had the US acted militarily against the Sandinistas, flights from staging areas closer to the action would have been far more practical. A KC-130 did support a nonstop transcontinental flight by a CH-53E on July 6, 1983, tanking the helo four times on its flight between Patuxent River, Maryland, and Tustin, California.

KC-130F 150014 of VMGR-352. *Robbie Robinson*

Also wearing the QB tailcode is BuNo 160015, one of the later KC-130R models, which is also seen at EI Toro. *Neil Dunridge*

The standard KC-130 finish for many years was a gray bottom and white top, divided by a black cheat line. In recent years, this has given way to a low-visibility two-tone gray scheme with toned-down markings. Some aircraft have also received self-defense systems, and lighting compatible with night-vision systems. Squadron VMGR-252 helped pioneer such operations, carrying out the first landing using night goggles in the spring of 1990.

Export sales of tanker-configured C-130s have also been made, as most foreign air arms that need tankers use the probe and drogue system. New-build KC-130Hs have been bought by the air forces of Argentina, Brazil, Israel, Italy, Morocco,

KC-130R 160013 (Lockheed construction number 4615) at Yokota AB, 1995. This aircraft was on the strength of VMGR-152 at the time. *Takanobu Okamura*

KC-130T-30 164597 of VMGR-452, one of the few stretched C-130s in US service. *Courtesy Paul Hart Collection*

KC-130T-30 4597, showing to good advantage the stretched fuselage. *Nick Challoner*

"Fat Albert" support transport of the Blue Angels aerobatic team, seen here in the early morning mist at RAF Finningley's "Battle of Britain At Home Day", September 1991. *Nick Challoner*

TC-130G "Fat Albert" making a fast fly-by at the US Air & Trade Show. *Chris Reed*

Side detail of KC-130T helicopter refueling pod. *Courtesy Paul Hart Collection*

Rear view of refueling pod. *Courtesy Paul Hart Collection*

KC-130T tanker/transport 163311 of squadron VMGR-452, part of the 4th Marine Air Wing. *Courtesy Paul Hart Collection*

Sistership 163592 is also on the strength of VMGR-452. *Courtesy Paul Hart Collection*

Tanker-configured Canadian CC-130H(T) of 435 Squadron. *Peter Davies*

Saudi Arabia, and Spain. Singapore had its quartet of C-130Bs (two ex-US, the others ex-Jordanian aircraft) refitted as tankers to support its F-5 force; Indonesia has carried out similiar conversions of some of its B-models. Additionally, since the retirement of their CC-137 tankers, the Canadian Forces now operate five CC-130Ts with Flight Refueling Ltd Mk32B underwing drogue pods, the tanker Herks coming under control of No. 435 Squadron at CFB Edmonton. A similiar program by Malaysia has added Mk.32B pods to a pair of that country's C-130Hs.

Herks for the RAF

The Hercules has enjoyed a prolific export run to air forces in every comer of the world, but Britain's Royal Air Force has been one of the more notable foreign users. The UK had been a potential C-130 export market since early on in the program, and it had been proposed to build versions of both the C-130C and GL-207 for the RAP. These plans came to nothing, and the service was planning for the introduction of the Hawker Siddely 861 V/STOL transport. However, this was one of the aerospace projects canceled in 1965 by a change in government, and later

Hercules C.3 XV223 in formation with unmodified sistership XV217. The stretch program did not increase the Herk's total payload capacity, but this was not the goal of the program, which was aimed allowing more bulky cargo to be carried. *LMASC*

RAF Herk carrying out a "Khe Sanh" landing. *Peter E. Davies*

C.1/C.3P refueling demonstration. *Peter E. Davies*

RAF C.1P XV292 with commemorative markings on the nose and the Union Jack on the tail. *Nick Challoner*

that year an order for C-130Ks (locally designated Hercules C.1) was announced. These would be based on the C-130E, as earlier plans to build a version with Rolls Royce Tyne turbo-props replacing the T56s had been turned down. However, a UK avionics fit was specified.

The first C-130K (XV176) flew on October 19, 1966, and entry into RAF service did not take long, the new aircraft being used to replace Hastings and Beverely transports. The No.242 Operational Conversion Unit at Thorney Island received the Hercules in April 1967, and on August 1st of that same year No.36 Squadron became the first operational unit. Originally, there were two squadrons at RAF Fairford near Bristol, one squadron in Singapore (No.48 Squadron, from October 1967), and another at RAF Lyneham. Reorganizations made Lyneham the central Hercules base, which it remains today.

The RAF remains the largest non-US operator of the Hercules, so it is not surprising that the service was the second air arm to rack up one million flying. hours with the C-130. This milestone was reached on March 27, 1990, with aircraft XV298, carrying a composite crew from all RAF Herk units.

RAF C-130s have worn a variety of paint schemes over the course of their history. While the first aircraft to be handed over had a natural metal finish, the first operational scheme consisted of sand and stone with black undersurfaces, optimized for desert operations. With the subsequent withdrawal east of Suez, a gray/green scheme was introduced, with the early light gray undersides later giving way to a wrap-around scheme. This in turn is being supplanted by an overall gray finish.

Like other air forces, the RAF had one major problem with the Hercules; the limited cross section that often led to the air-

Hercules C.1P XV306. *Courtesy Paul Hart Collection*

Mass fly-by of fifteen C-130Ks in July 1987. *Peter Davies*

craft being filled to its volume capacity with bulky cargo without reaching its weightlifting limit. This problem had already been addressed in the commercial world by the refit of early L-100s into stretched models, but the RAF would be the first military user of stretched C-130s. The C.3 retrofit program began in 1979, with the first conversion being carried out by Lockheed at Marietta. This aircraft first flew on 3 December 1979, and all subsequent conversions were handled by Marshalls of Cambridge in the UK. A total of thirty C.3s were converted, giving the RAF the airlift equivalent of an extra 89 standard C.1s.

Following the British withdrawal from many of its overseas military operations, the RAF's Hercules force, along with most of the British military was for the most part tasked with

C.1P XV306, as seen from XV211. The refueling probe is offset to starboard. *Neil Dunridge*

C.1P in the overall gray/green scheme, which replaced a similar scheme with gray undersides. The RAF's Herks originally wore sand/stone colors. *Neil Dunridge*

European operations in the NATO theater. Thus, it came as a shock when Argentina invaded the British-held Falkland Islands in 1983, provoking a war the UK's armed forces were not really prepared to fight. Among the difficulties that *Operation Corporate*, the campaign to retake the Falklands, posed was the remoteness of the islands themselves. The nearest airbase from which British land-based aircraft could operate was Wideawake Field on Ascension Island, thousands of miles away from the Falklands. The extreme distances, coupled with the RAF's inadequate number of refueling tankers spurred a number of improvised plans to extend the range of the Her-

cules force. First was the fitting of fuel tanks from Andovers in the cargo hold; aircraft with two of these tanks were given the C.1LR2 designation, while those with four were known as C.1LR4s. The extra fuel allowed long-range airdrop missions to the task force as it moved south, but even more capability was needed, and the internal tanks reduced the payload capacity.

More extensive were the refitting of C.1s as probe-equipped receivers and drogue tankers. The C.1Ps had fixed probes from scrapped Vulcan heavy bombers fitted, while six C.1K tankers each had a single Mk.17B hose-reel assembly fitted on the cargo ramp. The C.1Ks were too late for participation in the war, and could only refuel a single aircraft at a time. Nontheless, they provided a useful interim tanker capability, and supported postwar RAF Phantom operations in the Falklands, pending the arrival of new VC.10 and Tristar tanker conversions. The C.1ks were retired by the mid-1990s.

The Argentinian forces on the Falklands finally surrendered on 14 June, and within ten days RAF Herks were finally able to land at Port Stanley in support of the British reoccupation. Ironically, Argentina was also equipped with the Hercules, and made full use of its E- and H-model Herks during the initial invasion of the Falklands. Subsequently, the Argentine C-130s maintained an airbridge to the islands to keep the garrison resupplied, and continued to do so even after the Royal Navy arrived. Night missions to the islands were made at low level so as to evade detection by Sea Harrier CAPs, followed by short-field landings on the damaged airstrip at Port Stanley, which was the target of airstrikes by Harrier GR.3s

RAF Herk in the new gray scheme with a special non-standard red nose. Since the early 1990s, RAF types have been refinished in gray, with one C-130 very briefly testing an all-white scheme. *Neil Dunridge*

and Vulcan B.2s. One C-130H (either TC-63 or TC-66) was lost on June 1 while conducting a maritime patrol when hit by 30-mm cannon fire and an AIM-9 fired by a Sea Harrier. The final mission was flown on June 13, just prior to the surrender. The two Argentine KC-130Hs were also active during the war, in particular supporting the Exocet missile attacks carried out by the Argentine Navy's small force of Super Etendards.

Mention should be made of reports that RAF Herks even operated from the South American mainland during the war, flying from Chilean bases using false markings. These most likely performed missions in support of special operations teams that were observing Argentine airfields to give the fleet advance warning of raids.

After the war, Marshalls refitted the entire RAF Hercules fleet with refueling probes, save for W.2 XV208. This aircraft, operated by the RAP's Meteorological Research Flight, was converted by Marshalls as a platform for atmospheric and weather research. In order to accomodate a nose-mounted instrumentation boom, the weather radar was relocated to a pod atop the foward fuselage.

As not all older RAF Herks will be immediately replaced by the C-130J-30/C.4, a life extension program by Marshalls is underway, entailing the replacement of key longerons and other structural items. Other modifications have included putting US APN-169 Station Keeping avionics on twenty C.3s, and fitting Racal *Orange* Electronic Sensing Measures equipment on some aircraft, including four C.1k tankers. Countermeasures fitted to the RAF's Herk force have included ALQ-157 infrared jammers on the main gear blisters, and underwing AN/ALQ-66 warning recievers in pods.

Some RAF C-130Ks have been traded back to Lockheed Martin as part of the C-130J deal, and in late 1997 it was proposed to resell some of these to Angola, raising controversy within the US Congress.

CHAPTER TWO

Gunships

Certainly, the last role envisioned by Lockheed's designers when they were creating the Hercules in the early 1950s was that of armed combatant. Conceived of in an era when the first supersonic combat aircraft were entering service, the large, slow C-130 surely had little potential as a strike aircraft. However, little more than a decade after the YC-130's first flight, C-130 gunships were heavily engaged in a type of warfare that few had foreseen.

The idea of an aircraft with heavy gun armament for ground attack dates back to the First World War, and the US made extensive use of B-25 and A-26 gunships in World War II, Korea, and Vietnam. Although effective, forward-firing gunships could only keep their weapons on target during the run

in. An aircraft with side-firing weapons would be able to make pylon turns around a target, thus always keeping its guns pointed in the right direction. The concept had been evaluated as early as the 1920s, but no operational use of side-firing weapons on aircraft had yet been made. This began to change in the early 1960s, when the USAF was looking for more effective counterinsurgency aircraft, and tested under *Project Tailchaser* a Convair C-131 with a General Electric Minigun in the rear door. Using the same principle of operations as the Gatling gun of a century before, the Minigun used rotating barrels to permit very high rates of fire without causing excessive barrel wear. Flying in left handed circles around targets, the prototype gunship proved able to accurately lay down heavy fire, even with only one gun.

AC-130A 54-1630, *Azrael-Angel of Death*, of the USAF Reserve's 711th SOS during a visit to RAF Mildenhall on March 16, 1991. At that point, this aircraft had been in service for over thirty years, but still had almost a half decade of flying still ahead of it. It is currently on display at the USAF Armament Museum. *Robbie Robinson*

Clad in the post-Vietnam overall gray gunship scheme, A C-130A 53-3129 of the 711th SOS is seen here in June 1981. *Robbie Robinson*

Now the job was to produce an operational gunship, and deploy it to the deepening war in Southeast Asia. The ubiquitous C-47 "Gooney Bird" was chosen as the first gunship, as it was available in large numbers and its slow speed would not be a major detriment, at least over areas where enemy aircraft and heavy AAA were not present. Additionally, the C-47 could carry three Miniguns, and was already in use in Southeast Asia as a transport, flareship, and ELINT aircraft. C-47 44-8462 received a single Minigun, paving the way for "production" FC-47s with three guns, and by November 1965 the 4th Air Commando Squadron was operational in South Vietnam, where the "Spooky" gunships would more than prove their worth. The "fighter-Cargo" designation was soon abandoned in favor of the "attack" AC-47, which created less of a stir from "fast

mover" pilots. Operating at night over hamlets, airfields, and other installations, the AC-47s denied the Viet Cong the nighttime freedom of movement they had come to rely on. The terrifying red stream of 7.62 mm tracer fire suddenly appearing from above became the aircraft's signature, and US troops promptly named it "Puff, the magic dragon." A total of 53 AC-47s were converted; some aircraft were initially fitted with the well-proven and widely availible Browning .30-caliber machine gun in place of the scarce Miniguns, and the larger .50-caliber Browning also saw use.

Beyond defending hamlets, the US was also trying to interdict supplies coming down the Ho Chi Minh Trail system from North Vietnam, through eastern Laos, and into South Vietnam. This was demonstrated in early 1966 when AC-47s were

Port side view of an AC-130A fuselage, showing the 20-mm Vulcans and 40-mm Bofors. *Robbie Robinson*

Although having lost its guns, prototype gunship 54-1626 at the USAF Museum retains its southeast Asian paint scheme, Air Force Systems Command insignia, and three-bladed propellers. *Chris Reed*

Black Crow on -1626. Interestingly, the aircraft's data block still identifies it as a 'temporary test" JC-130A. *Chris Reed*

-1626's former fuselage cargo door area shows signs of the modifications made to house a pair of 20-mm Vulcan cannon in front of the landing gear fairing. This aircraft was originally flown with the short nose, but later received the APN-59 radar. The Black Crow is still fitted. *Chris Reed*

deployed to Udorn, Thailand, for antitruck missions over eastern Laos. The type's vulnerabilities became very apparent when used in this role, and by midyear several aircraft had been lost.

Clearly, what was needed was a larger gunship based on the C-130, which could carry more powerful weapons, more ammunition, night fighting-sensors, and have the fuel to stay on station longer. The Gunship II program was born out of these requirements, and the ASD team set about converting JC-130A 54-1626, making maximum use of existing systems and materials to speed up the process. Newer C-130Es were in great demand for transport use, but -1626 was one of the first production Herks, already a decade old, and was in use by the Air Force Systems Command, making it availible for the unorthodox project. Nicknamed "Super Spooky," the very first AC-130 had four XMU-470 Miniguns, with a pair each fore and

aft of the port landing gear blister. Arranged similarly were a quartet of M61 Vulcan 20-mm cannon. Like the Miniguns, the Vulcan was built by General Electric and used the same Gatling principle of operation. It was, however, much larger, and had been created as the standard cannon for US fighter aircraft. The prototype aircraft first flew in ASD colors, and had the early "Roman Nose," but was later refinsihed in a SEA-type scheme and was backfitted with an APN-59 radar.

While earlier gunships often relied on flareships, the AC-130s would be fitted with sensors for finding targets on their own. A starlight scope allowed targets to be spotted by amplifying the feeble light from stars and the Moon thousands of times over. A 20kw searchlight could also be used to provide illumination in the visible or infrared wavelengths. The searchlights were later downgraded to 2kw models, as these were less likely to attract heat-seeking SAMs such as the SA-7.

Rear fuselage antenna detail. *Chris Reed*

Port rear fuselage detail, showing the radome for the beacon tracking radar. *Chris Reed*

Forward fuselage antenna detail. The silver material inside the cockpit windows is to keep sunlight from raising the temperature inside so much that the windows burst. *Chris Reed*

54-1630 *Azrael* was sent to the USAF Museum after retirement, where it displays six camel and one crab mission markings from the Persian Gulf War. *Chris Reed*

ECM pod hung from the outboard pylon. During the Vietnam conflict chaff/flare dispenser were often carried on these positions. *Chris Reed*

-1626 retains JATO attachment points on the starboard side of the fuselage. *Chris Reed*

Steerable Xenon floodlight fitted in the rear port fuselage, obliterating most of the low-visibility "stars and bars." *Chris Reed*

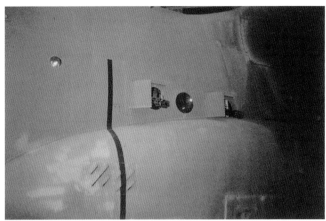

7.62mm miniguns fitted above the main gear blister. These weapons were often removed in later years due to their short range and lack of hitting power against hard targets. *Chris Reed*

Following the test period, 54-1626 arrived at Nha Trang Air Base, South Vietnam, on September 20, 1967. The first combat mission took place on September 27th, and on October 9th the crew first encountered truck traffic on the trail, and destroyed all six vehicles within fifteen minutes. This set the stage for the employment of additional AC-130s.

The only Herks availible at first for conversion were seven early JC-130As used as missile tracking aircraft at Patrick AFB, Florida, and so in December 1967 E-Systems was contracted to convert these Herks to Gunship II configuration. By June of 1968, the first of these aircraft, called *Plain Janes*, were complete. The *Plain Janes* had a number of detail differences from the prototype, including the fitting of a Texas Instruments Moving Target Indicator radar, and an AN/AAD-4 Foward Looking Infrared (FLIR) sensor made by the same company. Also, the computer was replaced by a Singer-General Precision unit.

Whereas the AC-47's basically defensive mission dictated that the aircraft be based in South Vietnam, the long-range AC-130 truck hunters were based at Ubon, Thailand, with the 16th Special Operations Squadron, which was at the time part of the 8th Tactical Fighter Wing. The unit was later redeployed to Korat prior to returning to the US

As the AC-130s entered service, the older gunships were gradually phased out. South Vietnam got twenty AC-47s, with Cambodia receiving six and Laos getting ten. The AC-119s were turned over to the South Vietnamese Air Force by late 1972, and some of these aircraft would be active until the fall of Saigon in 1975.

The first AC-130 to be lost was 54-1629, which was heavily damaged over Laos on May 24, 1969. The crew managed to get the stricken Herk back to Ubon, but it crashed on landing, killing two crewmen. 55-0029 *Midnight Express* was also to crash at Ubon, but was able to be repaired and returned to service.

Surprise Package

Aptly named, *Surprise Package* was aimed at producing a more effective AC-130A than the *Plain Janes*. The prototype Gunship II had been retained by the Aeronautical Systems Division as a test ship for future development, and in December 1968 ASD began reworking this aircraft as the *Surprise Package* demonstrator.

The *Surprise Package* configuration deleted the aft pair of 20-mm weapons, replacing them with two 40-mm Bofors cannon. Well proven as an antiaircraft weapon in WWII, the Bofors was by that time outmoded in its original role, but was still capable against ground targets, with a rate of fire of 120 rounds per minute. The *Surpise Package* aircraft flew combat trials in Southeast Asia between early December 1969 and late January 1970.

Pave Pronto

The success of *Surprise Package* paved the way for more gunships in this configuration. The AC-130 SPO began work on the *Pave Pronto* program in June 1970, with E-Systems serving as the installation contractor. By December of that same year, *Pave Pronto* AC-130As were deploying to Southeast Asia for combat duty. Surviving *Plain Janes* were sent back to the US to be reworked to the later configuration.

Another attempt at stopping the Communist road traffic by technological means was the AN/ASD-5 *Black Crow*, which was fitted to *Pave Pronto* aircraft from 1969. Mounted in a blister on the port side of the nose, *Black Crow* was a passive receiver, taking advantage of the fact that the ignitions of NVA truck engines produced radio frequency noise that could be heard and plotted.

The introduction of more intense antiaircraft threats over the gunship operating areas following the 1972 North Vietnamese invasion would claim several AC-130As that year. Aircraft 55-0044 *Prometheus* was downed by a SA-2 *Guideline* SAM over Laos on March 28, and on June 18 sistership 55-0043 was brought down by a SA-7 shoulder-fired missile.

The final AC-130 loss of the Southeast Asia conflict occurred on December 21, 1972, when 56-0490 *Thor* was lost over Laos to a AAA hit. Two of the crew managed to bail out and were rescued, but only one of the fourteen casualties was recovered, the other thirteen joining the ranks of the nearly 2,500 Americans declared as missing in action. A group of private US citizens searching for missing servicemen found the wreckage during a tour of Laos and Vietnam in September 1982, and two years later, the government of Laos agreed to a plan for a joint US/Laotian excavation of the site, the first such joint effort to investigate a crash location. The operation began in February 1985, with both US and Laotian soldiers clearing and then scouring the site. Remains were fragmentary, consisting of bits of bone and teeth; the crash had been quite violent, and the wreckage had burned for several days. Nonetheless, by July 1985 the remains had been identified by forensic analysis and returned for burial.

Following their Southeast Asia service, the surviving AC-130As entered Air Force Reserve service in the summer of 1976, equipping the 711th SOS at Duke Field, on the Eglin AFB reservation. The 711th was part of the 919th SOW, which until 1975 had been a tactical airlift group. The prototype aircraft - 1626 did not see postwar service, being retired to the USAF Museum at Wright-Patterson AFB in 1976.

A pair of AC-130As were already in Panama when the December 1989 invasion took place, and took part in the operation, covering the transports landing at Howard AFB as well as operating against Noriega's Panamanian Defence Forces. Although not immediately activated for duty in conjunction with the Persian Gulf crisis of 1990-91, the 711th did deploy several AC-130As in early February 1991. These are thought to have been based in Turkey. As late as September 1994 the AC-130As were still combat ready, and were standing by to provide cover for the US invasion of Haiti. Although the Haitian military had little heavy weaponry, there were 20-mm and 40-mm AAA sites that posed a danger to incoming C-130s and C-141s, so these were targeted for destruction. Despite the peaceful departure of the junta led by General Cedras and the subsequent cancellation of the invasion, the gunships still flew over Haiti as the occupation began, providing cover for convoys, surveying transportation routes, and deterring any possible hostile acts by the Haitian military.

By the mid-1990s the original gunships had reached the end of their lives. Now four decades old, they were becoming steadily harder to support, and the arrival of the new AC-130Us meant that they could finally be retired. The long-serving 53-3129 *First Lady* was preserved at the USAF Armament Museum, and *Ghost Rider* remains at Dobbins AFB, not far from the Lockheed plant where it was built. 56-0509 is displayed at Hurlburt's Air Commando Airpark in the SEA overall black scheme, while the cockpit section of 56-0469 *Grim Reaper* is in use as a ground trainer. The other survivors, 54-1627, -1628, 55-0011, -0014, -0029, and -0046 are stored at the Aerospace Materials and Recovery Center at Davis-Monthan AFB, Arizona.

Introduced during the Vietnam conflict, the AN/ASD-5 Black Crow sensor was carried by the AC-130As until retirement. *Chris Reed*

Starboard side scanner's position. *Chris Reed*

Pave Spectre: The AC-130E

Although the AC-130As were a major advance over the earlier gunships, they were limited by being based on old C-130A airframes which had performance penalties when compared to newer models. While earlier requirements had prevented the conversion of C-130Es, by the early 1970s sufficient numbers were availible to allocate eleven FY1969 E-models for refit into gunships, under the *Pave Spectre* codename.

Conversion of the C-130E airframes was carried out by the Warner Robins Air Material Area. The *Pave Spectre* AC-130Es had the same mission equipment as the *Pave Pronto* AC-130As, but their higher-rated engines allowed more armor to be fitted, as well as an increased ammunition load. Some AC-130Es were delivered in the SEA scheme with black undersides, but others were finished in an overall flat black scheme.

The steady upgunning of the AC-130s reached its pinnacle in 1972 with the addition of a 105mm howitzer under the *Pave Aegis* program. Familiar to Army artillerymen as a standard light towed artillery piece, the 105mm was chosen to give the AC-130s a definitive capability against even hard targets, such as armored vehicles. In the gunship role, the 105mm had a range of 12,000 meters, and with 5.6 lbs of explosive in a shell it was considerably more lethal than the 20 mm and 40 mm weapons. Including the 105mm in the gunship's arsenal entailed removing one of the Bofors to make way for the relocated side-looking radar. Modifications to the gun itself included adding a suppressor to keep the weapon's flash from giving away the aircraft's position. The howitzers were originally fixed, but a modification made them hydraulically trainable to allow easier targeting. The gun is in a raised position while the aircraft is on the ground to maintain clearance. The *Pave Aegis* refit was subsumed into the *Pave Spectre II* modification, which brought the aircraft up to C-130H standard with T56A-15 engines; the last several aircraft already had these uprated powerplants.

The AC-130Es additionally had the capability of designating targets for other aircraft. "Fast Mover" jet fighters were not well suited for finding and accurately hitting traffic on the trails at night, while the AC-130s, while far more accurate, were also more vulnerable thanks to their slower speed. In order to make the best use of both types the Pave Pronto AC-130As were fitted with AVQ-18 laser designators. Fitted beneath a ASQ-145 LLLTV camera, the designator could be used to mark targets detected by the IR and TV sensors, permitting precision attacks by F-4s with Paveway I "smart" bombs.

As the gunships increasingly had to deal with more advanced antiaircraft threats, various warning receivers and countermeasures were fitted. The AC-130Hs had a pair of antennas for the AN/ALR-46(V) system on the nose, and another pair

on the aft "beavertail." There was still no substitute for the human eye for spotting enemy fire, and the aft scanner was now given a plexiglass bubble in the rear ramp, a much superior alternative to being strapped to the lowered ramp, as on earlier aircraft. Another spotter's position was located on the starboard side of the fuselage, just above the foward part of the landing gear fairing. Countermeasures included dual AN/ALQ-87 ECM pods carried on pylons between the engines; the -87 was primarily a means of protection against the heavy SA-2 SAMs that were beginning to be emplaced along parts of the trails, and jammed the associated Fan Song guidance radar. On the outboard pylons SUU-42 dispenser pods could be hung, and AN/ALE-20 dispensers were also fitted. In order to provide an extra measure of crew protection, armor and ballistic curtains were mounted internally. Even with such defenses, the Spectres were far from invulnerable, as demonstrated when aircraft 69-6571 was shot down near the beseiged city of An Loc on March 30, 1972. This would be the only AC-130E lost in Southeast Asia, and thus the only one not to be rebuilt to AC-130H configuration.

The AC-130s were among the most potent of the many truck-killing aircraft deployed over the trail, but even the Spectres could not completely shut off the enemy supply traffic. Even hitting a truck did not necessarily mean that it was taken out of action, as many cargos did not burn or explode when struck. 40 mm ammunition with spark-producing liners and the 105 mm weapons produced more effective results, but new vehicles continued to pour in from eastern-bloc suppliers, and even more and better roads continued to be built.

Active combat for the Spectre force in Southeast Asia ended in the spring of 1973, but the AC-130s were still not quite through in Southeast Asia. On May 12, 1975, the American freighter SS *Mayaguez* was seized by Cambodian boats and its crew taken prisoner. A Spectre found the ship anchored near Koh Tang Island, where the crew was believed to be held. Gunships supported the bloody withdrawal of Marines from Koh Tang by Air Force HH-53s, following an abortive rescue mission. The gunships also destroyed several small Cambodian gunboats.

After the final USAF units left Thailand, the 16th SOS took its gunships to Hurlburt Field, Florida, where they remain today when not on deployment overseas. Like the AC-130As, the H-models were refinished in the overall gray gunship scheme. Refueling receptacles were added to allow increased range and endurance with tanker support, Today, the 16th is part of the 16th Special Operations Wing, a component of the Air Force Special Operations Command.

AC-130Hs were to have played a part in the Iranian hostage rescue mission, and had the operation not ended in disaster at Desert One, a trio of gunships would have covered the rescue, with one Spectre destroying the Iranian F-4 fighters on alert to prevent their interference, another flying over the former US Embassy itself, and another assisting in the seizure of the departure airfield. Certainly, the Spectres would have given the *Delta Force* rescue teams accurate and heavy fire support.

The next foes to feel the Spectre's firepower were Grenadan communist rebels and their Cuban allies, during the 1983 invasion. Hurriedly deployed to nearby Barbados, the gunships were among the first aircraft over the island. As reconnaissance coverage was lacking, it was not known that the runway at Point Salines was partially blocked until an AC-130 observed the field with its sensors shortly before the scheduled airdrop. The Grenadans and their Cuban allies were alerted to the US operation, and the gunships had to silence the unexpectedly heavy antiaircraft fire before the balance of the force could be dropped.

Another of the actions that went awry during the Grenada operation was the rescue of Governor-General Paul Skoon, who was being held captive in Government House. Navy SEALs freed Skoon, but were taken under fire, and were pinned down throughout the night. Fortunately, one of the Spectres was able to provide covering fire as needed until the team could be extracted the following day.

During the Reagan years of the 1980s, Central America became a major arena in the renewed Cold War, with the US seeking to bolster its allies in El Salvador and Honduras, while trying to undermine the Soviet-backed Sandinista regime in Nicaragua. During this period, AC-130H missions were flown over the region in an attempt to detect guerilla activity in El Salvador, and their supplies coming from Nicaragua. Disclosed in 1983, such flights were officially said to have been limited to Salvadoran airspace, but in reality may well have also ventured into Sandinista territory.

Upgraded AC-130Hs

Although the AC-130Hs were nearing twenty years of age by the mid-1980s, the type was judged to have sufficient life remaining to justify upgrading aging systems. Under a contract awarded in 1985, the Spectres were to be refitted with improved gun mounts, provisions for GPS, new HUDs, fire-control computers, FLIR, and encrypted communications gear. Flight testing of a refurbished gunship began in 1989, and the first aircraft was redelivered to the USAF on 31 July 1990. AC-130Hs have also been fitted with ALQ-172 jammers removed from retired B-52Gs. The gunships and other special operations Herks are prime candidates to be refitted with the ALE-50 towed decoy system, should this enter service.

In December 1989, five AC-130Hs were deployed from Hurlburt to Panama to participate in the Just Cause invasion, joining older AC-130As and a pair of H-models that were already in-country. The Spectres were invaluable for accurately attacking Panamanian forces in heavily built-up areas without causing collateral damage; targets included V300 armored cars and Soviet-built ZPU-4 antiaircraft guns.

The USAF special operations community was among the forces mobilized after the 1990 Iraqi invasion of Kuwait, and the deployment to the Persian Gulf area included four AC-130Hs. The gunships flew many missions following the start of the air war on January 17, 1991, including airbase defense flights and hunts for the elusive *Scud* ballistic missile launchers. But the most notable (and tragic) night of the war for the 16th was January 31. On January 29, the Iraqi Army had launched a cross-border operation against the Saudi town of Khafji, just over the Saudi-Kuwaiti border. The town had been previously evacuated, but Iraqi control over any Saudi territory was politically unacceptable, and the offensive came at a time when heavy US Army forces were out of position, redeploying to the west in preparation for Schawrtzkopf's "Hail Mary" attack. Thus, airpower, together with US Marines and Saudi and Qatari coalition forces had the responsibility of repelling Hussein's troops. In the morning hours of the 31st, three Spectres, nearly the whole force available in the theater, were assigned to support the allied counterattack, operating in shifts to maintain a constant presence over the battlefield. The first two aircraft were met with antiaircraft fire and artillery flares, but managed to take out some Iraqi armor before going off station.

Approximately a half hour before sunup, the third and final gunship, *Spirit 03* 69-6567 arrived on the scene. This crew destroyed a number of vehicles and Iraqi positions, staying in the area past daybreak to support Marines engaging the Iraqis. At around 0620 the aircraft was possibly about to break off and return to base, but by that time, the sun had been up for around a half hour, and whatever protection the darkness had provided was gone. The Iraqis were quick to take advantage of this, and *Spirit 03* was hit by a SA-16 *Gimlet* SAM, the missile's 2.7 lb warhead exploding a fuel tank in the port wing, taking it off. The 14-man crew never had a chance to get out, and the aircraft impacted into the waters of the Persian Gulf. At the time, the US military was trying to reveal as little information on aircraft losses as possible, to deny the Iraqis any intelligence on aircrews that might be trying to evade capture, and there was some confusion in the press over whether it was an AC or EC-130 that had been lost. Retrieval of the crew remains took place in March 1991, after the ceasefire.

Somalia and Yugoslavia

The Somali relief operation started out as a humanitarian effort, but within weeks of the US withdrawal in March 1993, the United Nations was clearly caught up in the renewed struggle between rival Somali factions that threatened to undo all the progress that had been made. On June 5, Pakistani soldiers belonging to the UN force were ambushed, and 23 of them were killed. The UN requested US aid, and six days after the attack three AC-130Hs were sent to the small African nation of Djibouti, within easy range of Somalia, in preparation for retaliatory strikes.

Targeted were installations to Mohammed Farah Aidid, whose forces were behind the attack on the Pakistanis. The Spectres were forward deployed to Mogadishu itself, and struck in the early morning hours of June 11. Working with Marine AH-1W Supercobra attack helos, the AC-130s attacked several compounds where Aidid's forces stored weapons, ammunition, and vehicles. Also, one of the gunships destroyed Radio Mogadishu, the warlord's private propaganda station. A pair of Spectres were assigned more Aidid-related targets on June 16th, but only one aircraft was able to carry out the mission, as the other lost a pair of engines shortly after takeoff and had to make an emergency landing. The Spectres were withdrawn from Somalia in mid-July, but almost immediately there services were needed elsewhere, namely the former Yugosla-

via, and by early August four aircraft were deployed to Brindisi, Italy.

The departure of the AC-130s from Somalia was ill-timed, as it stripped US forces on the ground in Somalia of some of their most effective close-support. Coupled with the decision of Defense Secretary Les Aspin not to send in M1 Abrams heavy tanks, this spelled trouble for the soldiers attempting to keep the peace between the warring Somali factions. On 3 October 1993 disaster struck, when an operation by Army Rangers to capture some of Aidid's key subordinates went awry. Caught in the urban confines of Mogadishu, the Rangers were pinned down by hostile Somali mobs, and two Blackhawk helos flying overhead were shot down by RPG fire. With no AC-130s or armor reinforcements on hand, the surviving Rangers could not be relieved until the next day, and TV audiences were subjected to the sight of Somali mobs dragging a dead US soldier through the streets. Although scores of Somalis were killed, US casualties were also high, with 19 killed and dozens wounded. Following the massacre of the Rangers, additional forces were deployed into Somalia to provide security for the US presence there; these reinforcements included several AC-130Hs.

Although based in Florida, the 4th SOS's AC-130Us are tasked with worldwide deployments. 89-0509 is seen here at Yokota AB, Japan. *Takanobu Okamura*

Although the Somali clans were never able to shoot down a Spectre, one gunship was lost near the end of US operations in the area. On March 14, 1994, Spectre 69-657, callsign *Jockey 14*, operating from Mombasa, Kenya, had a 105 mm round cook off in the cannon while on a training mission over the Indian Ocean. The gunship came down just off the coast of Kenya, and eight of the fourteen crewmembers were killed.

AC-130U: The "U-Boat"

When the AC-130E was created, it was thought that it would be the principal gunship until at least 1980. As things turned out, the *Pave Spectres* would serve in the frontline into the late 1990s. Despite the US withdrawal from Southeast Asia, the gunship was still seen as being valuable for certain tactical situations, where its firepower and precision outweighed its vulnerabilities. There was talk of producing a gunship version of either the YC-14 or YC-15, but the 1978 cancellation of the AMST program kept any such plans from coming to fruition. Some two decades after the first AC-130A flew, the Hercules was still an ideal basis for a gunship, as the C-130H airframe was well-proven and supportable, and by the late 1980s a whole new generation of sensors and fire-control avionics were

availible for gunship use. The USAF was to procure a dozen AC-130U gunships using new airframes fitted with mission equipment by Rockwell International. The arrival of the U-models would finally permit retirement of the long-serving AC-130As, with the AC-130Hs being shifted to the reserves.

The AC-130U is based on the previous gunship experience, but has much more capability than previous aircraft thanks to the sensor improvements. Central among these was the installation of the Hughes APG-180 synthetic aperture radar. Derived from the F-15E's APG-70 set, the -80 is capable of producing high-resolution SAR imagery of targets, as well as tracking ground beacons, ordnance impact points, and weather. Replacing the FLIR of earlier gunships is an All Light Level TV sensor which is fitted in a turret, allowing targets on all sides of the aircraft to be imaged. With this advanced computer/sensor integration, the AC-130U is the first gunship able to engage two targets simultaneously. Accuracy is also enhanced by plotting the aircraft and target positions with data from both GPS and inertial navigation systems.

The U-model retained the 105mm and 40mm weapons, but deleted the two 20mm Vulcans in favor of a single General Electric GAU-12 Equalizer 25mm cannon. Derived from GE's

Frontal view of 89-0509. *Takanobu Okamura*

Accompanying -0509 on its deployment to Japan was sistership 90-0165. *Takanobu Okamura*

earlier 30-mm GAU-8 Avenger, the GAU-12 is a trainable weapon with a 3,000-round supply of ammunition and a range of 12,000 feet.

To provide crewmembers and critical systems with better protection against small arms fire and fragments, lightweight ceramic armor is permanently fitted to sections of the airframe. Countermeasures include the AN/ALQ-172 jamming system mounted in the base of the vertical tail and in the upper fuselage, fuselage-mounted ALE-40 chaff/flare dispensers, and IRCM units on the wing pylons.

The first AC-130U flight took place in late December 1991, with the aircraft flying from Rockwell's Palmdale facility to Edwards AFB. The flight had been delayed due to software and wiring problems, and the first aircraft was not initially equipped with the ALLTV sensor system. Whereas production aircraft would be finished in a gray gunship scheme, the prototype had European I type colors.

Originally, the AC-130Us were to have equipped the 16th SOS, displacing the AC-130Hs to the reserves. However, the decsion to keep the H-models in active service led to the creation of the 4th SOS, which would be the user unit for the new gunships. The 4th was activated on May 4, 1995. The 4th is tasked with both European and Pacific duties, and on October 22-24 1997 the unit demonstrated its deployment capabilities by sending a pair of AC-130Us nonstop from Florida to Taegu Airbase, South Korea, for the US-South Korean exercise Foal Eagle. This marathon 8,000 mile mission required seven inflight refuelings from 14 ANG, AMC, and PACAF tankers, and took 36 hours.

There have been proposals to give the new gunships, as well as the older AC-130Hs, a forward firing armament by fitting AGM-114 Hellfires on the wing pylons, but to date this has not been done. Interestingly, this would not have marked the first time that a Herk had carried missiles, as a C-130A testbed was fitted with AGM-65 MAvericks in place of at least one of its external fuel tanks in the mid-1970s.

To date, no AC-130s have been exported, not surprising considering the cost and lethality of these aircraft. Following the Gulf War, Saudi Arabia was reportedly interested in having a small number of its Herks rebuilt as gunships, but nothing came of this. The RAF also considered having some of its surplus C-130Ks refitted to an AC-130U type configuration, but this too did not come to fruition.

Despite the procurement of a thirteenth AC-130U to compensate for the loss of an AC-130H in Desert Storm, there is still a shortfall of gunships in the USAF inventory, especially considering how heavily tasked special operations units have become. There has been some interest in converting one or more Air National Guard transport units to the gunship mission, but this has not yet occurred.

CHAPTER THREE

Special Operations C-130s

C-130E-I *Combat Spear*/**MC-130E** *Combat Talon I*

Following the Korean War, the USAF's special operations units were gradually cut back as the service concentrated on conventional and nuclear warfighting missions. However, by the early 1960s a new emphasis on "counterinsurgency" capabilities was in evidence, fueled by the growing number of guerilla-war type actions the US was finding itself involved in. A central-part of the special ops mission was the delivery and recovery of covert teams and supplies by aircraft, which had been pioneered by such units as the "Carpetbaggers" of WWII. A modern successor to the Carpetbagger's B-24s was needed, and the C-130 was the ideal basis for such an aircraft. Indeed, by that time, the Herk had already seen quite a bit of use in covert missions. The CIA "airline," Air America, had flown

Air Force C-130s with their markings removed in support of the Tibetan rebels fighting the Communist Chinese who had invaded their country.

The USAF's own dedicated force of special operations C-130s had its beginning with the 779th Troop Carrier Squadron, attached to the 314th TCW at Pope AFB, using modified C-130Es. Originally, the C-130E-Is were little different from standard E-models, the pivotal exception being the installation of the Fulton Skyhook Surface To Air Recovery system. Devised by Robert Fulton, Skyhook would allow a fixed-wing aircraft to recover personnel and/or equipment on the ground without landing. Basically, Skyhook worked by fitting the person or equipment to be picked up to a harness that was attached to a 450-foot line, the opposite end of which was brought aloft by a

C-130E 64-0571 was converted to the sole MC-130E-S model, without the Fulton gear. Seen here at Yokota AB during 1993, it was serving with the 1st Special Operations Squadron of the 353rd SOG. *Takanobu Okamura*

MC-130E-C fitted with the Fulton Surface To Air Recovery system's nose yokes. Finished in the European I scheme, this aircraft has a satellite communications antenna atop the fuselage; note also the pod under the pylon tank. *LMASC*

helium balloon. The recovery aircraft had fitted to its nose steel yokes that were folded back when not in use and opened scissor-fashion for pickups. Flying at 400 feet and 150kts, the object was to snare the line with the aircraft's yokes, which would then yank the pickup into the air. Lines running from the aircraft's nose to the wingtips prevented a missed line from fouling the propellers. Dual pickups were also possible, with the first being done at Edwards AFB in May 1966. Not all the C-130E-Is were Skyhook-equipped; aircraft so modified were

MC-130E-C doing a Fulton demonstration, with the nose-mounted arms in the open position. The cables running from the nose to the wingtips are to protect the propellers in case the pickup cable is missed. In this particular case, the cable (thankfully, not attached to a person) broke when snagged. *Nick Challoner*

later termed MC-130E-C "Clamps," with the balance being MC-130E-Y "Yanks" and a single MC-130E-S "Swap." The Fulton system was phased out of use in 1996, with a *Combat Talon* of the 8th SOS making a final series of pickups at Hurlburt on September 16th of that year. The distinctive Fulton "whiskers" remained on skyhook-equipped aircraft until the summer of 1998, when they began to be removed and stored.

Vietnam was the obvious locale for the first operational use of the Skyhook aircraft. The deployment of a small detachment (*Stray Goose*) to Ching Chang Kuan, Taiwan, was carried out in the summer of 1966. CCK was the base of the 314th Troop Carrier Wing, to which the detachment belonged, but operational missions (*Combat Spear*) were carried out from Nha Trang, South Vietnam. Nha Trang was a center for special operations in the theater, also hosting Army *Green Beret* forces.

Whether or not operational use was ever made of the Fulton system remains a question, even thirty years after the Skyhooks went into action. Officially, the USAF has said that no combat retrievals were made. This may not be accurate, as the circumstances of the loss of 64-0547 in late December 1967 remain clouded, and it has been reported that the aircraft had been engaged in Fulton operations when it was lost. The crash site is known to have been in Laos, but the fatal damage may have been incurred over North Vietnam while making a pickup. The crash killed all eleven of the crew; the wreckage site was found in the early 1990s. Prior to the loss of -0547, another aircraft had been destroyed by mortar fire at Nha Trang on November 25, 1967. Both losses were replaced by new conversions.

MC-130E-C 64-0561 in the new special ops scheme in 1994, still retaining the Fulton gear. *Nick Challoner*

There were several redesignations during the unit's time in Southeast Asia: The first came in March 1968 when it became the 15th Air Commando Squadron. That November, the Air Commando nomenclature was phased out and the unit became a Special Operations Squadron. Although continuing to fly Southeast Asian missions, the C-130E-Is were moved to Kadena AB, Okinawa, in the spring of 1972. In December of that year, the unit's designation was changed to the 1st SOS, which had until November been used by the last USAF A-1 unit. Postwar the 1st was based for years at Clark AB, Phillipines, but since 1991 the unit has again been based at Kadena as part of the 353rd SOG, although it was reequipped with the MC-130H *Combat Talon II* in October 1995.

The MC-130E designation was applied to the former C-130E-Is in the late 1970s, with the "M" prefix designating USAF special operations aircraft. Confusingly the Navy uses the same prefix for minesweeping aircraft. The Vietnam era black and tan scheme eventually gave way to European I colors prior to the introduction of a new special ops scheme in the 1990s.

Precision navigation is obviously crucial for the special ops mission, and the *Combat Talons* were fitted with extensive navigational aids, including a FLIR, high-definition mapping radar, INS, and LORAN-C. Other modifications included fitting the aircraft for airdropping at speeds up to 250 knots, a full 100kts faster than the limit of standard C-130s. Countermeasures included an AN/ALR-46 warning receiver to detect radar threats, AN/ALE-27 chaff dispensers, and the AAQ-8 IRCM system. And by the late 1970s, nearly half of the force had been reengined with C-130H-type T56-A-15 engines in place of their original -7s. Originally, a number of MC-130Es were fitted to carry underwing drogue pods for refueling heli-

MC-130E-Y 63-7785 (Lockheed construction number 3852) at Yokota. *Takanobu Okamura*

Full view of 63-7785. *Takanobu Okamura*

A solitary Fulton-equipped MC-130E among other *Combat Talons* retaining the standard C-130E nose radome. *LMASC*

copters, but this capability has now been added to all *Combat Talon Is*, permitting them to supplement the MC-130P *Combat Shadow* force as necessary. In 1996, it was announced that the AN/APQ-122(V)8 radars of the Talon fleet would be upgraded by Texas Instruments, the original contractor for the system.

MC-130E operations in the NATO theater (*Combat Arrow*) were the responsibility of the 7th SOS. The post Cold War drawdown of USAF forces led to a reshuffling of units, with the 7th being relocated to RAF Alconbury, UK, as part of the 352nd SOG.

With the arrival of the new MC-130Hs, some E-models have been shifted to the reserves, with the 711th SOS of the 919th SOW at Duke Field, Florida, taking charge of a pair of *Combat Talons* in October 1995 as replacements for its AC-130A gunships. There have been several peacetime Talon losses, with the first taking place on December 5, 1972, near Myrtle Beach, South Carolina, when 64-0558 collided in midair with a F-102A Delta Dagger. And in February 1981, 64-0564 was lost near the Phillipines.

Mid-section view of 63-7785. *Takanobu Okamura*

Rear view of aircraft 73-1582 (Lockheed construction number 4544) at Yokota in 1992. This aircraft is a very early C-130H; essentially a C-130E with T56A-15 engines. The 21st Airlift Squadron of the 374th Airlift Wing used three of these "Super Es" (73-1582, -1597, -1598) for *E-Flight* missions. *Takanobu Okamura*

"Super E" 73-1598, another of the E-Flight aircraft, seen here landing at Yokota. *Takanobu Okamura*

Following Vietnam and *Operation Eagle Claw*, the next combat action seen by MC-130Es was the *Operation Just Cause* invasion of Grenada in October 1983. The Talons' main role during the operation would be landing US Army Rangers at the Point Salines airport. Obstruction of the runway complicated matters, as it had been planned to airland the majority of the Ranger force, following the airdrop of a team at 0500 to secure the immediate area. Fighting their way in through bad weather, three MC-130s made the run over Salines, but only one aircraft managed to drop its load, putting a lightly armed headquarters unit on the ground that was pinned down until the balance of the force could be landed.

During *Operation Just Cause*, the December 1989 invasion of Panama, the 8th SOS contributed three MC-130Es to the operation. These took part in the airdrop on the Rio Hata barracks of the Panamanian Defense Forces, where some of the PDF's elite troops were housed. Prior to the drop, a F-117 dropped a pair of laser-guided bombs into a field nearby, in the first combat use of the "stealth fighter." This was claimed to be a deliberate miss intended only to stun and disorient the PDF troops. While this was done, Army Rangers dropped to engage the PDF battalions. Following Noriega's surrender to US forces on January 3, 1990, a MC-130E crew of the 8th got the job of transporting the former strongman and his captors from Panama to Miami, Florida, for incarceration pending trial.

MC-130H *Combat Talon II*, **in European I colors.** *Courtesy Paul Hart Collection*

At least four *Combat Talon Is* from the 8th were deployed to the Persian Gulf in 1990 to conduct unconventional operations against Iraqi dictator Saddam Hussein's forces. Th leaflet dropping mission was resurrected, showering Iraqi forces in Kuwait with millions of leaflets promising fair treatment to surrendering soldiers. Another, more active bit of "psyops" saw the Talons drop 11 BLU-52 "daisycutter" Fuel Air Explosive bombs, these huge weapons having a tremendously demoralizing effect on the dug-in Iraqi troops.

In contrast to the Combat Talons' usually secretive duties, on July 10, 1998, MC-130E 64-0566 carried out a highly-visible mission, namely the transport of the remains of 1st Lt. Michael Blassie, the former Unknown Soldier of the Vietnam conflict, from Dover AFB, Delaware, to Scott AFB, Illinois, for burial after the body had been examined and identified. The 8th SOS's involvement in this mission was due to the fact that Blassie was a member of the squadron when he was killed in May 1972 while flying an A-37.

Operation *Kingpin*: The Raid on Son Tay

The November 1968 bombing halt of North Vietnam spelled the end of regular US combat operations over North Vietnam, but did nothing to secure the release of hundreds of Air Force and Navy aircrews being held as POWs. It was known that the prisoners were subject to all manner of deprivation, from brutal interrogations to starvation and disease. Although President Nixon was committed to getting the US out of an active combat role in Southeast Asia, there was also a stong incentive to get back the imprisoned US personnel, some of whom had been in Communist hands since 1964.

Although they were being held deep within North Vietnam, the POWs were not all kept in a central facility, such as the infamous Hoa Lo, known as the "Hanoi Hilton." A number

MC-130H nose radome detail. *Chris Reed*

of smaller camps had been created to handle the captured Americans, and these were vulnerable to heliborne raids. Although not all prisoners could be brought out short of putting thousands of troops on the ground, even rescuing a portion of the POWs was seen as being worthwhile. It would certainly save the lives of some, and returned servicemen could attest to the barbarous treatment of their former captors, hopefully countering North Vietnamese propaganda and US domestic support for the communists.

The prison at Son Tay was chosen to be the target. Located some thirty miles to the west of Hanoi along the Son Cong River, Son Tay was estimated to hold at least 70 POWs and was defended by only a light garrison, although of course thousands of NVA troops were based in the general area, and the site was well within the umbrella of air defenses.

Planning for a rescue mission began in August. The ground combat contingent would consist of 56 Army Special Forces "Green Berets," commanded by Lt. Colonel Arthur "Bull"

BLU-82 Daisy Cutter on display at the National Museum of the USAF. The final operational BLU-82 was expended by an MC-130E over Utah in July 2008. *Chris Reed*

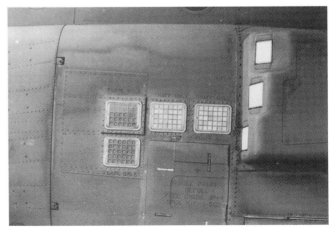

MC-130H chaff/flare dispensers. *Chris Reed*

Combat Talon II satellite communications antenna. *Chris Reed*

Dorsal "towel rack" antennas of an MC-130H. *Chris Reed*

Simons. Aided by SR-71 and drone imagery, precise models of Son Tay were produced for orientation and planning, and rehearsals began using a full-scale mockup at Duke Field on the Eglin AFB reservation. Preparations were rapid, and the mission was ready to go on one of two "windows" in October and November.

The go-ahead for the operation was given by President Nixon on November 18, and the rescue force launched from Udorn, Thailand, on the night of November 30. The Special Forces assault force was carried by five USAF HH-53C Super Jollies, which would also carry back any rescued prisoners. A smaller HH-3E Jolly Green would also be brought along, to be landed in the confined courtyard of the prison. Two HC-130Ps (callsigns *Lime 1 & 2*) were detailed to refuel the helos, and a C-130E-I was to act as pathfinder. Close-in support around Son Tay itself would be taken care of by five Air Force A-1 Skyraiders (callsigns *Peach 1-5*). As related in Frederick A. Johnson's *Douglas A-1 Skyraider: A Photo Chronicle* (Schiffer Publishing), these A-1s may well have been specially equipped to carry precision-guided weapons. Another C-130E-I served as a leadship for the Skyraiders; both of the "Blackbirds" had just received infrared sensors for better navigation at night. The helos had to be refueled over Laos, a difficult enough task, given the low level nighttime flight. This was compounded by the fact that the HH-3E was less powerful than the larger Super Jollies and was thus harder to bring into position behind the tankers.

The C-130s, helos, and escorts were not the only aircraft over North Vietnam that night. In order to keep the North Vietnamese air defense grid looking away from the raiders, Navy carrier aircraft carried out mock strikes, while USAF F-4Ds and F-105s stood by-to provide protection against MiGs and SAMs, respectively. In all, over 100 aircraft were involved in the operation.

Upon arriving in the vicinity of the camp, the C-130E-Is dropped pyrotechnics designed to mimic the sounds of a firefight, as a distraction. Also dropped were napalm canisters, to guide the helo crews to the prison. One of the difficulties faced by the Son Tay raiders was the presence of a military training camp to the south that from the air resembled the prison. As luck would have it, one helo did end up landing at this site mistakanly, and Berets aboard engaged the NVA troops and Chinese advisors stationed there before rejoining the main force.

Despite the unscheduled diversion, the balance of the raid went as planned, with the Berets quickly neutralizing North Vietnamese resistance. However, once inside with cutting torches and other tools, ready to free the POWs, the troops found to their horror that there were no American prisoners; it was later determined that the POWs had been moved some months previously due to flooding. Without anyone to bring back, the Berets departed Son Tay on the HH-53s, the whole assault taking under half an hour.

Given the risks inherent in such a mission, US casualties were extremely light. There were a pair of relatively minor injuries among the ground troops; in the air, a pair of F-105 Weasels were hit, but one managed to make it to safety in Thailand, while the other crew was rescued by HH-53s after punching out over Laos. The HH-3 had to be destroyed by an explosive charge, but this had been anticipated.

Disaster at *Desert One*

Certainly, the blackest day in the history of US special operations forces is April 24, 1980, the date of the abortive mission to rescue 53 US hostages being held by the revolutionary government of Iran. Publicly, the US followed a diplomatic course, hoping that sanctions and negotiations could secure the hostages' release. Behind the scenes, however, there was from early on in the crisis intensive planning for a military rescue mission.

Various plans for a raid on the former embassy in the capitol city of Tehran eventually gelled into *Operation Eagle Claw*, with the role of actually breaching the embassy falling to the Army's newly created *Delta Force* counterterrorism unit. The group's commander, Colonel Charlie Beckwith, had been an active proponent of unconventional warfare and anti-terrorist capabilities for years.

Eagle Claw was truly a multiservice affair, a fact that would greatly complicate planning and training, and would also be a factor in the mission's ultimate failure. Transporting Beckwith's men to the *Desert One* forward base in the Iranian desert some 250 miles from Tehran would be the job of three MC-130Es, operating from the Omani island of Masirah. Once on the ground in Iran, they would rendevous with eight Navy RH-53D Sea Stallion helos, stripped of their minesweeping gear and flown by Marine pilots from the carrier *Nimitz* in the Indian Ocean. the *Delta Force* troops would board the helos, which would be refueled on the ground by three EC-130Es carrying fuel bladders in place of their usual ABCCC command capsules. The C-130s would then leave Iran, while the assault force would be taken to a final staging area closer to Tehran. The following night, following a ground infiltration of the city, a strike would be launched on the former embassy. The RH-53Ds would pick up the team and released hostages and take them to Manzantkiyeh, where a force of Army Rangers would have secured the field to allow a pair of C-141 evacuation aircraft to land.

The MC-130s and fuel birds successfully landed at *Desert One*, guided in by remotely-activated beacons installed in early April on a survey mission by a CIA Twin Otter. However, the helicopters were having a much harder time of it. An unpredicted "haboob" or dust storm was encountered, which rapidly cut visibility down to nothing. The C-130s had also encountered this, but their superior navaids permitted them to get through it. The RH-53s were not so fortunate, and to make matters worse one aircraft experienced a loss of blade pressurization, which forced the crew to land and abandon their craft, being picked up by another helo. Two others had to land for a time due to the lack of visibility before pressing on, and yet another had to abort the mission and turn back to the *Nimitz* when its artificial horizon system went down.

Finally, an hour after their planned ETA, the remaining helos reached *Desert One* and the waiting C-130s. The helicopter aborts still left the force with six RH-53Ds availible, which was the minimum number required to carry on to Tehran. However, one helicopter had made it in with one of its hydraulic systems inoperative, which ruled out taking it any further along. The decision was made to abort, and preparations were made for departure, with the aircraft being loaded and the helos made ready to refuel for their trip back to the *Nimitz*.

As the helicopters hover taxied into position, sand was thrown up into the air by rotors and propellers, rapidly cutting visibility down to nearly nothing. Disaster struck when one of the RH-53s hit the left side of the EC-130 it was attempting to refuel from. There was an instantaneous explosion, and the night was lit by a major fire. The three-man crew of the helicopter died, as did the EC-130's aircraft commander, copilot, two navigators, and the flight engineer. The others aboard the Hercules managed to escape, but the aircraft were total losses, being engulfed in an inferno of burning fuel and exploding ammunition.

Any hope of a textbook exfiltration ended with the collision. It was decided that the RH-53s would be abandoned rather than refueled, given the loss of one of the tankers and the fact

HC-130P 64-14855 of the Air Force Reserve, a former HC-130H still retaining its Fulton type nose in the summer of 1994. *Nick Challoner*

HC-130P 66-0225 in Systems Command garb refueling an Army MH-47 Chinook. *LMASC*

that the remaining C-130s were themselves running low on fuel. The plan had in any case called for the helicopters to be destroyed at Manzariyeh, but in the chaos at *Desert One* the destruction was not carried out for fear that exploding helicopters might cripple one or more of the C-130s. Likewise, it was not possible to recover the fatalities due to the intense fire.

Despite the catastrophe, the Iranian military never detected the US activity on its territory, and did not reach Desert One until the following day, after the mission's failure had been announced by President Carter. Once on site, the Iranians made use of their propaganda windfall, parading the world press past the intact RH-53Ds (complete with sensitive documents), the C-130/helo wreckage, and the badly burned bodies. The remains were subject to a grisly exhibition in Tehran before being returned to American custody.

YMC-130H *Credible Sport*

Immediately after the catastrophe at *Desert One*, planners began preparing for a new rescue mission, should one be ordered. The main plan crystallized under the codename *Honey Badger*, and would have been a far more ambitious operation than *Eagle Claw*. The Meharab International Airport in Tehran would have been seized by Army Rangers to serve as a base, with nearly 100 USAF and Army helicopters being flown in aboard C-5s. The helos would take rescue teams to the now-scattered hostages, while AC-130s provided close support and Navy F-14s dealt with any interference from the Iranian Air Force.

Whether *Honey Badger* could have succeeded where *Eagle Claw* failed must forever remain in the realm of speculation, as the followup operation was never launched,-and the hostages were freed in the early hours of the Reagan Adminstration

in January 1981. However, there was yet another rescue mission in the planning stages during the summer and fall of 1980, one centered around the use of a highly modified C-130.

Codenamed *Credible Sport*, the YMC-130H was an engineering feat, created by Lockheed Georgia within a matter of weeks. The type of rescue that the aircraft was created for was to be far smaller in scope than *Honey Badger*, but much more unconventional. A single aircraft would be used both to bring the rescue team to Tehran, and to fly the team and recovered hostages to safety, operating not from a conventional airfield or even a rough strip or road, but a soccer stadium near the former US embassy.

Preparing the Hercules for such ultra-STOL operations was no small task, but Lockheed managed to do it in short order. Rocket assistance for both the takeoff and landing phases of flight was absolutely essential, but these would have to be much more powerful than the standard 1,000-lb thrust RATO units. Accordingly, eight Mk6 motors were fitted for blasting the aircraft out of the stadium. Eight forward facing motors from Navy RUR-5 ASROC antisubmarine rockets were used to decrease the landing run, with six other ASROCs being fitted for pitch/yaw control, and eight motors from AGM-45 Shrike missiles would buffer the landing.

The *Credible Sport* modifications were in no way limited to the fitting of rockets. A terrain following radar was mounted in a stretched nose radome similar to that of the drone control models, with a FLIR turret underneath. Airframe modifications included enlarging the ailerons, flaps, and leading edge extensions, and installing the horsal and dorsal surfaces fit proposed for the Amphibious C-130. Aerial refueling would be necessary, so a refueling receptacle similar to that of the C-141B was fitted above the forward fuselage. The cockpit would also receive lighting compatible with the use of early generation night vision goggles.

The *Credible Sport* contract was let on July 29, 1980, with the first flight taking place exactly two months later. Three C-130Hs (74-1683, 74-1686, and 74-2605) were put through the refit, although only -1683 was fully converted. On October 29, 1980, 74-1683 took off on what was to be the first all-up test flight, from one of the auxiliary fields on the Eglin reservation. Just prior to landing, the forward facing rockets were accidentally fired while the aircraft was still airborne, bringing the YMC-130H to a dead stop; the resulting crash knocked a wing off, but the crew managed to get out safely.

Of the surviving *Credible Sport* aircraft, 74-1686 was never returned to service, and is now on display at Warner Robins AFB, Georgia. 74-2605 was brought back to C-130H standard, and at the time of writing was still in service at Dyess AFB, Texas. The DoD and USAF have to this date not released any details on the *Credible Sport* operation, although the basic details of the aircraft and its proposed mission were rumored for some time. Video footage of the test program was acquired by Jane's, and revealed publicly on 3 March 1997.

MC-130H *Combat Talon II*

Although the buildup of US strategic forces during the early Reagan era of the 1980s garnered the most public attention, the much more shadowy world of special operations was also a beneficiary of increased military spending. Envisioning that the US would often find itself in conflicts where conventional military operations would be tactically or politically impracti-

cal, special operations advocates worked hard to secure funding for new equipment, especially aircraft.

Among the new types needed was an updated *Combat Talon*, as by the mid-1980s the MC-130Es would be reaching twenty years of age, and in any case, additional aircraft would be needed to meet growing commitments. Planning for the *Combat Talon II* program originally centered on fitting two dozen new C-130H airframes with the basic MC-130E mission equipment. However, major advances in avionics and sensor design allowed better, more modern systems to be fitted, producing a much more capable aircraft.

The MC-130H was the first special operations C-130 derivative to be built new, thus giving all 24 aircraft a higher degree of commonality, and permitting a better fit for mission equipment. Externally, there are many changes between the *Combat Talon IIs* and earlier models. The little-used Fulton system was never fitted, and the nose contour was changed to house the Emerson (later Electronic & Space Corp's) AN/APQ-170 radar. This set has a single processor driving two transmit/receive antenna systems; one a X-band unit for terrain avoidance, and back to back Ku-band antennas for 360-degree ground mapping, beacon location, and weather mapping. Both the X- and Ku-band systems can operate simultaneously, and either can take over the role of the other, albeit at reduced performance.

The design of the MC-130H took advantage of lessons learned from the original *Combat Talon* program, the YMC-130H *Credible Sport*, and the C-130H/"C-130X" testbed 83-1212. Additionally, much of the special avionics were based on those developed for the canceled HH-60D Night Hawk.

HC-130N 69-5823 carrying out a refueling of an HH-53 over Mildenhall in 1980. *Robbie Robinson*

69-5823 in ARRS colors. *Robbie Robinson*

On the flight deck, the *Combat Talon II*'s avionics permit flights in all weather conditions at altitudes of 2,250 feet or less. Terrain following is accomplished by cues from both the X-band radar and the Texas Instruments FLIR, mounted in a turret underneath the nose. The radar/FLIR combination is also used during airdrops and approaches into austere fields.

A total of seventy-five troops can be carried by the MC-130H compared to the MC-130E's limit of fifty, this increase being attributable to the removal of the navigator and radio operator positions from the cargo hold. Like the *Combat Talon I*, the MC-130H is equipped for high speed airdropping, with panels being fitted around the ramp to serve as air deflectors.

Training for flight crews transitioning to the MC-130H (as well as other special operations C-130s) is provided by the 58th SOW at Kirtland AFB, New Mexico. Part of the Air Education Training Command, the 58th has a single fixed-wing component, the 550th SOS, equipped with *Combat Talon IIs* and MC-130P *Combat Shadows*.

In recent years, the danger from new-generation shoulder-fired SAMs such as the US Stinger and the Russian SA-14 has increased as these weapons have proliferated worldwide. USAF special operations C-130s have for some time carried underwing Northrop QRC 84-02A pods to protect against such threats, the pods emitting energy in the IR band to distract missile sensors. To counter advanced missiles capable of all-aspect attacks, an improved version, the QRC 84-02B, was proposed in the early 1990s. This would have a turret on the pod containing an IR sensor and two IR projectors. When cued by a MAWS such as the AAR-44 that an attack was un-

derway, the pod sensor would acquire and track the incoming missile, directing the IR beams directly against it. Like the AC-130U, the *Combat Talon II* is also fitted with the ALQ-172 jamming system, originally developed for the B-52.

Although there is no way to make an aircraft with the C-130's radar and infrared signature "stealthy," efforts are underway to lower the vulnerability of special operations models that have to operate in contested or enemy airspace. Infrared suppressor "tubs" have been in use for years, but these have a detrimental effect on fuel consumption, and thus new methods of reducing the considerable heat signature of four T56 engines are being investigated.

The USAF is looking to procure a new generation of helicopter refueling pods for the *Combat Talon II* force; this is a priority as the older tanker-configured MC-130E/Ps will be reaching the end of the lifespans not long after the turn of the century. The transport capability of these aircraft will be replaced by CV-22 Ospreys, but these will not have tanker capability. There has been talk of buying an all-new low observable "MC-X" transport/tanker designed from the outset for special ops work, but given the rundown of the defense budget, this is a long-term prospect at best. The new pods would differ from the 1960s-vintage equipment used on the older aircraft, having digital controls and lighting compatible with night vision systems. Aside from refueling helos in the air, tanker-equipped MC-130Hs could also serve as ground refueling points at forward airstrips.

The Pacific-based Talons of the 1st SOS at Kadena; Okinawa, have as one of their major contingencies the role of

MC-130P 69-5832, a former HC-130N now dedicated to the refueling of special operations helicopters and other covert tasks. The dorsal blister has been removed. *Nick Challoner*

operating into North Korea should hostilities recommence on the Korean peninsula, and the unit has a forward operating location at Osan AB in South Korea.

Three MC-130Hs from RAF Alconbury were the first aircraft available for airdrop missions during the Rwandan relief operation, *Support Hope*, and within two days of going into action, the *Combat Talon IIs* had airdropped 17 tons of relief supplies. Another MC-130H of the 352nd participated in the unsuccessful search for survivors from a C-141B/Tu-154 collision off Africa in September 1997. MC-130H operations over the former Yugoslavia have included flights in the fall of 1996 by the 7th SOS to transport delegates during postwar elections.

HC/MC-130P *Combat Shadow*

The first Hercules tanker version for the USAF, the HC-130P, came about as a result of early combat rescue operations in Vietnam. Although helicopter rescues of downed airmen had taken place as early as World War II, during the war in Southeast Asia such missions became commonplace, and many aircrews escaped death or capture when a rescue helo plucked

Sistership 69-5833 remains a HC-130N, based in Florida for rescue work. *Nick Challoner*

them from behind enemy lines. In an effort to extend the range and endurance of helicopters operating deep within North Vietnam, the USAF looked into the possibility of fitting its new HH-3s with aerial refueling capability. Tanking helos from the large, high-speed KC-135 tankers was clearly impossible, but a tanker based on the C-130 and equipped with drogue refueling pods could possibly refuel helos fitted with probes. The first air-to-air helicopter refueling was accomplished on December 17, 1966, when a Marine KC-130F carried out trials with a USAF CH-3C fitted with a refueling probe, paving the way for procurement of twenty HC-130Ps, which were built with the drogue pods. A prototype JHC-130P was converted from one of the last HC-130Hs, and also carried out early air refueling tests.

The use of air-refuelable helicopters was seen by some as a stopgap measure until a V/STOL aircraft with high speed and long range could be developed specifically for combat search and rescue. Various proposals were looked at, including designs with stowed rotors, but none were ever built, and the "interim" helos would become the standard CSAR vehicles. The CH-3Cs were superceded by the HH-3E version, and eventually the much larger HH-53B/C Super Jolly

In one of the first demonstrations of the capabilities of the new system, a pair of HC-130Ps supported the nonstop flight of two HH-3Es from New York to Le Bourget, France, for the 1967 Paris Air Show. The helos tanked nine times along the 4,157 nm course, which followed the route taken by Charles Lindbergh.

The HC-130Ps were followed by fifteen HC-130Ns. These did not have the Fulton system fitted and thus had "regular" noses, but the dorsal blister was still present, and the aircraft were fitted with direction-finding equipment.

In April 1986 a pair of HC-130Ns from the 67th ARRS/ 39th ARRW at RAF Woodbridge in England were deployed to Naples, Italy, in preparation for Operation El Dorado Canyon, the joint USAF/US Navy airstrikes on Libya. Supporting a trio of HH-53Cs, the HC-130Ns stood by to assist with search and rescue operations; unfortunately, these could not recover the crew of a F-111F downed in the strike, which was the only aircraft lost.

Combat Shadows from the 9th SOS operated from Saudi Arabia during the Gulf War, supporting helos conducting combat search and rescue and special operations into Iraq and occupied Kuwait. In the opening hours of *Desert Storm*, HC-130s refueled the MH-53Js that had guided the AH-64s of *Operation Normandy*, the strike that took out pivotal Iraqi early warning radar sites. 67th SOS HC-130s from the UK were also active in the war, taking part in *Operation Proven Force*, the northern front operating from Turkey. The *Combat Shadows* flew from Batman Airbase, supporting the *Pave Low* helos based there. A similar role was played out several years later by HC-130s based at Brindisi, Italy, serving as tankers for the MH-53Js that provided SAR coverage for NATO aircraft operating around the former Yugoslavia.

The 5th SOS of the 919th SOW is the USAF Reserve operator of MC-130Ps, being activated on January 7, 1995, and

HC-130H(N) 88-2102 of the New York ANG's 102nd Rescue Squadron at Fairford on July 21, 1996. *Robbie Robinson*

taking charge of the first of its *Combat Shadows* in May of that year.

In February 1996, those *Combat Shadows* tasked with special operations became known as MC-130Ps, with those dedicated to air rescue work remaining as HC-130Ps. The Shadows were formerly among the least well equipped of the Special Operations Command fleet, but are receiving updates to bring their capabilities more in line with other MC-130 models. Modifications include the special cockpit lighting necessary for the use of night vision devices, refueling receptacles to allow tanking from KC-135s and KC-10s, GPS, and secure communications.

During *Operation Assured Response* in April 1996, *Combat Shadows* flying from Sierra Leone refueled Air Force *Pave Lows* and Army Special Operations Chinooks that were evacuating Americans and others from unrest in neighboring Liberia.

A HC-130P of the USAF's 304th Rescue Wing at Portland, Oregon, was lost on a training flight over the Pacific on November 22, 1996. The aircrew reported electrical problems and the loss of one engine shortly before contact was lost; subsequently, the other T56s also failed and the aircraft glided for a time before impacting the ocean surface. A hour and a half after the aircraft went down the Coast Guard found and rescued the sole survivor. The HC-130's wreckage was later located by the Navy, and the aircraft's "Black Box" flight recorders were retrieved from over 5,100 feet of water by a USN deepwater salvage vessel.

CHAPTER FOUR

Special Use and Testbed Models

DC-130

The US military has been using radio-controlled target drones for gunnery training since World War II, but the postwar introduction of missile armament increased the need for such training. Although many different drone designs have been produced over the Years, one of the more successful has been the Ryan (later Teledyne Ryan) Q-2/BQM-34 Firebee. The Firebee was designed from the start for either ground or air launch, and after early tests from B-17s, the B-26 Invader became the standard launch aircraft. However, by the late 1950s, the Invaders were getting long in the tooth, and the USAF began looking for a replacement. The C-130A was ideal, as it had plenty of lifting power, and could carry four underwing pylons, as op-

posed to the B-26's two. Two C-130As were adapted as drone carrier/launchers, with the first taking to the air in April 1959. The designation GC-130A was at first applied to these aircraft, as the USAF used the "G" prefix to designate parasite aircraft and their motherships. Two pylons were fitted underneath each wing, and a stretched nose was fitted with a small turret underneath. This was necessary to accommodate the antenna for a microwave command system that allowed controllers aboard the C-130 to remotely control the drone.

Although created for a training mission, the C-130/drone combination would in the 1960s take on a wartime role. The recon drone program had its start even before the loss of Gary Powers and his U-2 over Russia on May 1, 1960. Seeking a

The prototype DC-130H, with four of the advanced BQM-34s on underwing pylons. The aircraft is also identifiable by the extended nose radome, with an undernose turret which contained an antenna for remote control of the drones. Using advanced computer controls with time-sharing features, the DC-130H could simultaneously control all four BGM-34s. *LMASC*

DC-130 on the line at U-Tapao, Thailand in 1971. *Kenneth R. Middleton*

reconnaissance vehicle that would cause less political turmoil than a manned aircraft if shot down, it was proposed to build a recce version of the BQM-34, designated Model 136 and codenamed *Red Wagon*. Funding would instead go to Lockheed's A-12/SR-71 project, but the drone concept remained alive. The later *Lucy Lee* proposal was for a drone to conduct standoff reconnaissance missions at altitudes of better than 65,000 feet following a DC-130 launch. This got no further than *Red Wagon*, but in February 1962 a contract was let to produce the first four Model 147A recon drones. Codenamed Firefly, the 147 was a stretched version of the Firebee, with extra fuel and provision in the nose for cameras. This version would form the basis for an entire family of intelligence-gathering drones.

Although programmed before launch, the drones could also be remotely "hand flown." Versions with TV cameras could also relay imagery back to the DC-130; aside from aiding in navigation, this also allowed "real time" collection of images. If a drone managed to make it out of hostile airspace, it was directed to a recovery area by a pilot-rated Drone Recovery Officer. The preferred method of recovery was a mid-air snag,

which was the mission of specially-equipped CH-3 helos. Once over a recovery zone, the drone's engine was shut down, with the "bug" descending under a tail-mounted drag chute to 15,000 feet where a larger 100-foot parachute (attached below a 24-foot chute) was deployed. Flying over the descending drone, the CH-3 would snare the top parachute with three hooks. The main chute would then be released, and hydraulic winches aboard the helo would be activated, first allowing the line to play out, and then bringing the drone back up, to within 200 feet of the helicopter. If this was successful, the helo would then transport the AQM-34 to a recovery base, where the exposed film would be removed for processing and interpretation, while the drone itself was refitted and refueled. Despite the dangers of mid-air recoveries, exacerbated by the ever-increasing weight of the drones and the hot southeast asian environment, the helo crews were overwhelmingly successful in their mission, with an effectiveness rating of nearly 98%.

The DC-130/AQM-34s' first operational missions were against Communist China in August 1964, as by that time SA-2 sites were a threat to CIA/Taiwanese U-2 operations over the mainland. During these early operations, there was only a single

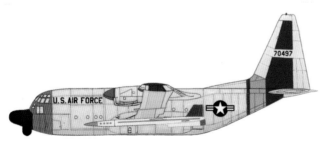

DC-130A 57-0497 early in its career, with a Northrop Q-4B supersonic target drone. Later transferred to the USN, this aircraft is currently on display on "Celebrity Row" at AMARG. *Chris Reed*

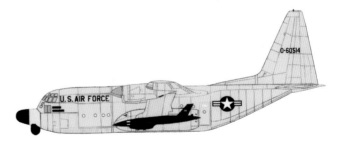

DC-130A 56-0514, prior to being transferred to Navy control. This aircraft was scrapped after retirement, although the fuselage was retained as a movie prop. *Chris Reed*

The AQM-34Ls were based post-Vietnam at Davis-Monthan AFB, hence the "DM" tailcode. Note the endplates fitted to the tail of this version. *John M. Sepp*

AQM-34L wing attach point detail. *John M. Sepp*

command station availible, and thus there could only be one recovery area, in Taiwan. That same month, however, skirmishes to the south in the Gulf of Tonkin between US destroyers and North Vietnamese torpedo boats finally brought the US into that war, and the DC-130s were deployed to Bien Hoa AB, South Vietnam. Lack of adequate support at the base necessitated a move back to Okinawa, but by October the unit had returned to Vietnam, marking the start of what would be more than a decade of operations over the region. On February 11, 1966, the parent 4080th Strategic Wing became the 100th Strategic Reconnaissance Wing, and the 4025th SRS was redesignated as the 350th SRS. Supplementing the DC-130As from 1967 were seven DC-130E conversions. These more powerful aircraft could carry the inboard fuel tanks, increasing their operational flexbility. The prewar high-visibility training markings were abandoned, replaced by more sinister SEA

camoflauge, and the drones themselves were finished in low-visibility colors.

The drone operation was highly classified, but knowledge of it became an "open secret" when the Communist Chinese began publishing photos of AQM-34s shot down over the mainland. Ironically, decades later the Chinese themselves would use an AQM-34N copy for photo recon work, even using a Tu-4 *Bull* refitted with turboprop engines as a mothership. This later gave way, ironically, to a Y-8/An-12 *Cub*, the Soviet-designed counterpart to the Hercules.

Drone operations ran the gamut from low altitude sorties (where power lines and even vegetation were hazards) to missions at 65,000 feet. Accordingly, there were different drone variants for the different requirements. High-altitude missions were undertaken by the long-span (32-foot) AQM-34P optimized for daytime photo recon, the similar AQM-34Q *Combat*

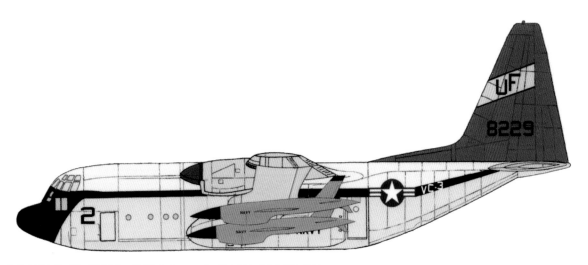

DC-130A BuNo 158829 of VC-3, formerly C-130A 56-0491. This aircraft lacked the "Pinocchio" nose radome. *Chris Reed*

Underside view of the first XQ-2C Firebee prototype, now on display at the NMUSAF. Powered bya Continental J69 turbojet, this drone flew 25 missions before being retired in 1960. *Chris Reed*

Dawn with data-linked sensors and underwing fuel tanks for extended range, and the AQM-34R. The AQM-34M was a single drone fitted to drop expendable ELINT receivers while in flight, these relaying data on enemy radars as they fell to earth. Although capable of carrying four Firebees on target missions, the DC-130s were restricted to a pair of AQM-34s, as the extra equipment fitted to the recon "bugs" made them heavier than their predecessors.

An early mission for the drones over North Vietnam was the *United Effort* program, aimed at gathering data on the Soviet-supplied SA-2 *Guideline* SAM system. Vietnam would be the first time that US forces would encounter SAMs in combat, aside from the U-2 losses of 1960 and 1962, and electronic intelligence on the system was vital if means were to be found to counter it. Drones were obviously the safest way to gather such information, and thus some models were fitted with traveling wave tubes to augment their radar signatures. This made them appear to North Vietnamese radar operators as U-2s and provoked SAM firings. When fired upon, the drones ELINT gear relayed data on the SA-2's *Fan Song* radar via a data link to RB-47II Stratojets flying outside of enemy airspace. The concept was not new, as the Model 147D drone had been been built for such missions over Cuba, although it was never used in this role. A similar program was carried out in the fall of 1972, during Operation *Linebacker*, the renewed air offensive against the north.

Aside from the sorties over North Vietnam and Communist China, North Korea was also a target for drone operations. On April 18, 1969, North Korean MiGs shot down a US Navy EC-121M in international airspace over the Sea of Japan while the converted Super Constellation was conducting an ELINT mission. Coming little more than a year after Kim Il Sung's military had seized the spy ship USS *Pueblo*, this incident showed that US recon platforms were at high risk around the

Korean peninsula. The losses prodded the development of an unmanned ELINT type that would not put lives at risk in the area. Ryan modified the high-altitude photo reconnaissance Model 147T as the Model 147TE *Combat Dawn*, with external fuel tanks and remotely-controlled COMINT receivers that could relay intercepted communications through a data link. The *Combat Dawn* missions were flown from Osan, South Korea.

Beyond the workhorse Model 147/AQM-34 series, DC-130s also served as motherships for more exotic drones. The Model 154/AQM-91A was an early attempt at producing a stealthy vehicle, with smooth lines, inwardly-canted tails, and a General Electric YJ97 engine mounted atop the fuselage to minimize the radar/IR signature. Much larger than the -147, the 154 had wings 48 feet in span and a fuselage 34 feet long. Missions were to be carried out with IR and ELINT systems, as well as Itek KA-80A panoramic cameras. It was planned that the AQM-91 would succeed the AQM-34 and manned U-2s for flights over mainland China, with its,extreme operating

Tail detail, showing this version's bulbous antenna. *John M. Sepp*

Flying at altitudes of 35,000 to 40,000 feet, NASA's NC-130B was used to conduct global earth surveys, suing a variety of sensors to map global resources. These measurements provide a detailed low-altitude supplement to satellite coverage. *LMASC*

Nixon put an end to such plans, and the AQM-91 never saw use.

C-130s were to have played another drone support role in Asia, namely the mid-air recovery of film capsules from D-21B drones. The strategic reconnaissance D-21Bs, originally designed for air-launching by A-12 Blackbirds, were flown a few times from B-52Hs, the mission profile calling for the drones to make Mach 4 flights over denied territory (prinicpally communist China), subsequently ejecting the camera/film section over the Pacific for retrieval by JC-130Bs.

Many drones were shot down by North Vietnamese AAA, SAMs, and MiGs during the war. However, this was small a price to pay for the millions of photographs brought back, and in any case, no aircrew were lost when a drone was downed. The AQM-34s proved to be hard to destroy, given their small size, speed, and ECM. Ironically, one drone was shot down by a quartet of Navy F-4 Phantoms after they had mistook it for a MiG-21 attempting to intercept the controlling DC-130! The drones occasionally turned the tables on pursuing MiGs, running them out of fuel or leading them into "friendly" AAA and SAM fire. When hit, the -147s proved capable of making it back with large amounts of damage, and thanks to their modular construction could often be rebuilt.

In all, the 350th flew 3,435 drone missions in Southeast Asia, with the loss of 578 "bugs" to enemy action. Missions were flown even after the US combat role ended, and drones imaged the final NVA drive into South Vietnam.

Tactical Air Command Use

Although many pilots in the USAF hierarchy were loathe to consider drones even as supplements for manned aircraft, there were combat roles beyond reconnaissance that the "bugs" were well suited for. One of these was electronic warfare, with the

altitude and low-observability characteristics protecting it against SAMs and MiGs. Due to their larger wingspans, only two AQM-91s could be carried by a DC-130, on the outer pylons. The detente with Mao's regime established by President

The RAF Meteorological Flight's rather modified C-130K Hercules W.2 XV208 at the International Air Tattoo, RAF Fairford, July 1994. *Nick Challoner*

Some two decades after having been converted to DC-130H standard, former HC-130H 65-0979 is seen here at Edwards on 21 October 1995. Now designated as a NC-130H, -0979 serves with the 514th Test Squadron. *Neil Dunridge*

drones being equipped as jammers and chaff layers to protect manned aircraft.

Thus, TAC's 11th Tactical Drone Squadron was activated at Davis-Monthan AFB in the summer of 1971. This unit primarily flew the AQM-34G (Model 147NA/NC) with underwing ALE-2 chaff dispensing pods. Development of this variant had begun prior to the bombing halt of November 1968, as a means of coping with the increasingly potent North Vietnamese antiaircraft grid. Although denied their original mission, some TAC drones were deployed to Southeast Asia to participate in *Operation Litterbug*, the dropping of leaflets over North Vietnam, supplementing similar missions made by C-130E-Is.

There were even plans to use the drones in an active attack role against enemy defenses, in particular SAM sites. Under the *Have Lemon* program, a small number of BGM-34A/Model 234s were converted to evaluate procedures for launching weapons from RPVs. The drones conducted successful trials with AGM-65 Maverick missiles and Hobos guided bombs, but these did not lead to an operational system.

Postwar, SAC gave up drone operations and the AQM-34s were turned over to TAC's 432nd Tactical Drone Group at Davis-Monthan AFB. The 22nd Tactical Drone Squadron, with four DC-130Es, flew photo-recon missions with AQM-34Ls (both LORAN and TV models) and newer AQM-34Ms. The

JC-130B 57-0528 of the Air Force Systems Command, showing the distinctive dorsal fairing for direction-finding antennas. *LMASC*

Aircraft 57-0526 was the second C-130B, and was converted to JC-130B satellite retrieval configuration. It is seen here with the recovery apparatus deployed. *USAF via Edwards AFB History Office*

Low-level shot of 57-0526, accompanied by a T-28 Trojan chase plane. *USAF via Edwards AFB History Office*

11th TDS continued to be tasked with electronic warfare missions with its five DC-130As and AQM-34H/V drones.

The Vietnam experience was still fresh when Lockheed was contracted to rebuild a HC-130H as the first DC-130H. Planning for future RPV growth, the H-model could carry four drones of up to five tons each. In July 1976, the DC-130H set a world turboprop external weightlifting record at Edwards AFB by taking aloft a quartet of drones weighing a combined total of 44,150 lb. The primary drone intended for the new aircraft would be Teledyne Ryan's BGM-34C, a major upgrade of the AQM-34 series developed to give TAC a standard drone that

could be rapidly fitted for different missions. The electronic warfare role would see the -34C fitted with no fewer than five jammers in the nose, plus a pair of underwing ALE-2 or ALE-36 pods to dispense chaff. Photo recon missions could be flown by fitting a nose equipped with a KS-170 camera, and the new drone could also be used in the attack role, carrying two AGM-65 Mavericks underwing.

Just as the USAF's drone operation was set to gain new capabilities with the DC-130H and BGM-34C, the entire program met with a premature end. There were always elements within the USAF with a bias against unmanned aircraft, and

WC-130H 65-0963 is one of those former HC-130Hs to retain the Fulton style nose, although the dorsal blister has been deleted. *Courtesy Paul Hart Collection*

even among some drone supporters there was recognition that the DC-130 launch/mid-air recovery profile was not ideal. The 11th and 22nd were deactivated in April 1979.

Following the USAF drone program's demise, some AQM-34L/Ms were put into storage, being brought back into service during the late 1980s to help test new air defense radars. AQM-34Ls were used to simulate enemy missiles during testing of FPS-124 North Warning Radars in Alaska and Canada, while AQM-34Ms played a similar role for the Over the Horizon-Backscatter (OTH-B) radar in Maine. During the OTH-B tests, launches from C-130s were made from the vicinity of Puerto Rico. Use of the AQM-34s allowed the USAF to evaluate the new radars' ability to spot small targets, as the drone's size was close to that of the new Soviet AS-15 Kent Air Launched Cruise Missile.

Nearly fifteen years after the end of the recce drone program, a similar project, again using the Firebee as a basis, sprang briefly from the ashes. The driving force behind the Argus program was the USAF's complete lack of real-time tactical reconnaissance capability. TV-equipped AQM-34s had demonstrated the basis for such a capability many years before, but by the late 1980s the Air Force was still relying on the RF-4C Phantom II with film-based sensors. This proved to be a major problem during Desert Storm, as by the time recon films had been developed and disseminated, they were often so outdated as to be worthless. A crash program codenamed *Argus* saw Teledyne Ryan refit Firebees to a reconnaissance configuration with film-based sensors and TV cameras for relaying near real-time intelligence. *Argus* was not ready before the end of Desert Storm, but development continued, and a pair of drones participated in USAF exercises. Despite this, further development of an *Argus*-derived system was not pursued, the USAF instead preferring to concentrate on the Martin Marietta ATARS for installation on RF-16s and new Teledyne-Ryan BQM-145 RPVs. Ironically, ATARS itself was later canceled in favor of new Unmanned Aerial Vehicles.

Navy Drone Launchers
The US Navy has also made use of DC-130s for launching drones, as targets for both fighters and missile-equipped ships. The focal point of such operations is the Pacific Missile Test Center, headquartered at Point Mugu, California. DC-130As 55-0021 and 56-0491 were transferred to USN control in 1969, becoming 158228 and 158229, respectively. Additional aircraft were later transferred and used by squadron VC-3, allowing retirement of the unit's DP-2E Neptunes. Today, active DC-130As are maintained and flown for the Navy by the private firm Avtel, the former VC-3 unit having been disestablished. The camoflage paint schemes have given way to "high viz"

colors for maximum visibility. The venerable Firebee continues in use in the BQM-34S form. Unlike the USAF's recon drone operations in Southeast Asia, mid-air recovery of the Firebees is not done at PMTC. Instead, at the end of their missions the drones are lowered by parachute to the ocean surface where they float until located and retrieved by NCH-46 Sea Knight helos.

Navy DC-130As have also played a role in the development of a new generation of unmanned aerial vehicles. In November 1995, DC-130As airlifted (internally) a detachment of Predator UAVs to San Nicolas Island off the coast of California for trials. The drone launcher Herks have always had a secondary transport mission, with the interior equipment being removable.

Falling Star
Well before the CIA's U-2 operations over the USSR came to an abrupt halt on 1 May 1960, work was well underway on a photo reconnaissance satellite that could image Soviet targets from the near invulnerability of low earth orbit. The original Air Force WS-117 project was absorbed into the CIA's *Corona* program, and working under the cover of the *Discoverer* project, Lockheed designed a vehicle based on the Agena upper stage that was sent into orbit atop a Thor missile. This would form the basis for the first-generation of spy satellites.

Although it had been hoped to produce a system that could relay imagery in real-time to ground stations, television-type sensors of the time could not produce the necessary resolution. Film-based cameras could do so, but this meant that the film had to be ejected from the satellite after exposure, and deorbited in a reentry vehicle. Obviously the retrieval of the film capsules was of critical importance, and a small number of C-119s were fitted to snag the capsules in mid-air, following reentry and parachute deployment. Finally, a C-119J caught the *Discoverer XIV* capsule southwest of Honolulu, Hawaii, on August 19, 1960, but it was obvious that a more powerful aircraft was needed for the task. Accordingly, six C-130Bs were withdrawn and fitted for use by the 6594th Test Group/6593rd Test Squadron at Hickam AFB, Hawaii. HC-130H/P aircraft were also used by this squadron.

WC-130H 65-0985. *Peter E. Davies*

Reentry of capsules was staged over the Pacific, with radio beacons guiding the C-130s, which were equipped with direction finding gear in dorsal blisters, to them. Upon making visual contact with a capsule's parachutc, a C-130 crew would attempt to snag the chute with a grappling line from the opened cargo bay. If successful, the line would then play out and a winch would bring the capsule into the bay.

Testing of the retrieval system was carried out by the Air Force Satellite Control Facility's Operating Location 1, based at Edwards AFB, California. OL-1 evaluated retrieval systems, aircraft, and satellite systems. During testing, one aircraft would drop a simulated reentry capsule from approximately 30,000 feet, with the retrieval aircraft flying some 12,000 feet lower, waiting for the capsule to descend.

The JC-130Bs were later replaced by four NC-130H aircraft fitted for the retrieval mission. This role was finally phased out with the retirement of the last "bucket dropping" US satellite, the KH-9 "Big Bird." The final attempt to launch a KH-9 took place in April 1986, and the 6594th was deactivated that same year.

Satellites were not the only objects to be snatched from the air by C-130s. In April 1966 it was disclosed that a HC-130 had snared an AIR-2 Genie rocket after it had been fired by a F-4C Phantom II flying over White Sands, New Mexico. Fitted with instrumentation in place of its usual nuclear warhead, the Genie had reached 150,000 feet. HC-130 recovery aircraft also figured into the USAF's PRIME (Precision Reentry Including Maneuvering) program, which flew subscale X-23 lifting bodies atop Atlas missiles to test ablative heat shields and reentry profiles. The first two PRIME missions, on December 21, 1966, and March 5, 1967, resulted in the vehicles being lost, but the final flight on April 19, 1967, was successfully caught. This sole surviving X-23 is now on display at the USAF Museum.

MAFSS Firefighters

The commercial Hercules airtankers are not the only C-130s used to fight forest fires, as several ANG squadrons and a single USAF Reserve unit have this as a secondary mission during the fire season. In the early 1970s the US Forestry Service and the USAF developed the Modular Airborne Fire Fighting System (MAFFS) which could be rapidly fitted to standard C-130s. The proof of concept prototype, tested onboard a C-130A in 1971, differed in a number of ways from later units, having the discharge nozzles fitted in the paratroop doors, and only two retardant tanks. The production MAFFS incorporates a series of five tanks that fit in the aircraft's cargo bay, a pair of dispenser nozzles fitted on the cargo ramp, and control equipment. MAFFS can hold 3,000 gallons of retardant, which is

dyed to aid in firefighting coordination, and contains nitrates, allowing it to act as fertilizer for post-fire regrowth. With its large capacity, the C-130 is classed as a "Type 1" tanker; only a limited number of aged C-97s and a pair of even older Mars flying boats have more capability.

Military firefighting aircraft have retained their standard paint schemes, although temporary high-visibility numbers and bands are applied to make the C-130s stand out in the dark, smoky skies above fires. The missions, however, are still risky; in May 13, 1995, a Hercules from the 302nd Airlift Wing at Peterson AFB, Colorado, crashed near Bliss, Idaho, while returning from a MAFFS mission on a fire near Boise, killing all six crewmembers.

In October 1997, the Wyoming ANG's 153rd AW deployed three C-130s, two of them equipped with MAFFS, to Indonesia to combat the massive forest fires raging throughout that country. Some 250 missions were flown before the aircraft re-turned to the US in December. Although this was called the first oveseas deployment of USAF MAFFS aircraft, firefighting C-130s had in fact been sent to Italy in the 1970s. Italy itself now has MAFFS units; other overseas-operators include Australia, Portugal, and Greece.

NC-130A ASETS

Following the retirement of the AC-130As in the fall of 1995, the sole C-130A in US military service is NC-130A 55-0022, appropriately nicknamed *Lone Wolf*. Flying with the 40th Flight Test Squadron at Eglin AFB, Florida, -0022 is part of the Airborne Sensor Evaluation Test System program. The aircraft is equipped with a retractable 50-inch diameter turret under the fuselage, aft of FS245. This can house a variety of sensors for tracking weapons, aircraft, or making atmospheric measurements; sensors can include FLIR, millimeter-wave radar, video, and film cameras. Despite its age, by July 1997 *Lone Wolf* had only 8,750 hours on its airframe, which is not judged to be excessive for an aircraft more than forty years of age. The NC-130A's long-term future is uncertain, although a Periodic Depot Maintenance scheduled for 1998 will keep it airworthy until 2003 at least.

C-130C/NC-130B Boundary Layer Control Testbed

Of the US armed forces, only the Army does not operate the Hercules. This is not to say that such use has not been considered, as during the early 1960s the service was considering the procurement of its own force of V/STOL attack aircraft and assault transports. The Hercules was picked as the basis for a STOL airlifter, and aircraft 57-0712 was converted to NC-130B configuration as a prototype for the projected C-130C production version. YT56-A-6 engines were fitted in underwing pods,

C-130 carrying temporary dayglow tanker numbers. These are applied on firebomber missions to make the dark military C-130s stand out; civilian airtankers have permanent high-visibility paint schemes. *Courtesy Paul Hart Collection*

these providing additional airflow over the flaps and control surfaces when needed. Additional alterations included a larger rudder and wider-chord ailerons, and a 22-foot braking parachute. In this configuration the NC-130B could operate fully loaded from 1,400-foot fields. The first flight in this new configuration took place on February 8, 1960.

Despite the success of the flight tests, no orders were ever placed for C-130Cs, as Army plans for a large fixed-wing force came to naught. Although having been evaluated with Army use in mind, the NC-130B was flown in USAF markings. Following Air Force use, the NC-130B was transferred to NASA as N929NA, later N707NA. Losing its pod-mounted engines, the aircraft flew as part of the Earth Survey II program. A slightly extended nose radome was fitted during this period. Supplementing satellite coverage, this provided low-altitude imagery for comparision, and was used to cover the aftermath of the Mount Saint Helens eruption. The Herk's multispectral sensing capability came into use when it was used to survey western wildfires, looking through smoke to chart the progress of blazes.

Weather Reconnaissance

One of the more important peacetime roles of the Hercules has been its use as a meteorological platform, including use as a "hurricane hunter," taking sensors into and around tropical storms and hurricanes to provide data on their strength and direction. The first storm penetrations were flown in 1943 by an AT-6 Texan trainer, and such flights would become a valuable tool in the days before weather satellites, providing coastline communities with at least some warning of impending storms. In the early postwar years, a variety of aircraft types were flown on weather missions, with converted WB-29s playing a major role until 1955 when B-50s released from SAC service were

pressed into use as WB-50Ds to replace the older Superfortresses. By the early 1960s the WB-50s were nearing the end of their useful lives, and their replacements would be five WC-130Bs (62-3292/96), these being the last C-130Bs built. Additionally, aircraft 58-0731 was used as a WC-130B by the US Weather Bureau as N6541C. The USAF aircraft entered service in 1963, and flew the penetration missions while WB-47E Stratojets were used for high altitude flights around the periphery of storms. Since the retirement of the Stratojets, WC-130s have been the primary USAF meteorological aircraft, along with a smaller number of WC-135Bs. The new-build WC-130Bs were supplemented by twelve transport conversions; WC-130 user units included the 53rd, 54th, and 55th Weather Reconnaissance Squadrons. The WC-130Bs were followed by six WC-130E conversions, which served until the mid-1990s

The US gulf coast is one of the regions that is hardest hit by tropical storms, and due to the speed which storms can cross the Gulf of Mexico, warning time is essential. Hurricane Camille of 1969 struck the coast and killed dozens in the southern US, and this helped to create pressure to base the WC-130s in the gulf coast area to provide better coverage. This was done in 1973 when the 53rd WRS set up shop at Keesler AFB, Mississippi.

More active measures against storms were also attempted; codenamed Storm Fury, flights were made to seed hurricanes with silver iodide crystals in an attempt to defuse their energy. These missions proved capable in some cases of slowing and reducing storms, but could not eliminate them.

WC-130H

A total of 16 HC-130Hs were rebuilt to weather reconnaissance configuration as follow-ons to the WC-130B/Es. Some of these later conversions retained the dorsal radome, while others kept the Fulton-type nose. Two aircraft have since been converted to HC-130Ns, another pair to C-130H configuration, and a single example has become an MC-130P *Combat Shadow*.

Most hurricane penetration missions last approximately 11 hours; with their cargo bay tanks the WC-130Hs have a total endurance of some 14 hours. Storm penetrations are made at 10,000 feet, with the object being to provide forecasters with measurements of conditions 100 miles out from the center of the storm, and get four fixes on the center itself from different approaches. Typically, penetrations are made every six hours, but storms closer in to land can merit more frequent observation. The WC-130 airframes are not reinforced for their special mission, but penetrating the eyewall of a hurricane is no trivial matter, with the aircraft being subject to wind shear, driving rain, and low visibility.

The WC-130Hs are equipped to dispense dropsonde weather sensors, and a Dropsonde System Operator is part of the crew. Upon being dropped, a dropsonde deploys a small parachute and gathers information on barometric pressure, wind velocity and direction, humidity levels, and temperature as it falls, relaying the data back to the DSO via a HF radio channel. Rate of descent of the dropsondes is approximately 1,000 feet per minute. The position of dropsondes is fixed by means of Omega navigation receivers, but these are being replaced by more accurate GPS systems. Besides dropsondes, WC-130s also occasionally drop buoys that measure wind speed and direction from the surface of the ocean. As many as four of the 700-lb buoys can be dropped on a single mission, from the opened cargo door.

Going into hurricanes is actually only part of the job for meteorological aircraft. WC-130s are also tasked with conducting low-level missions into potential tropical depressions to determine if a low-pressure area is beginning to form a rotating storm. And in the winter storm season flights are made to track the "nor'easters" that periodically dump large amounts of snow on the eastern US.

By the late 1980s, the USAF was attempting to do away with the hurricane hunter mission, claiming that satellites could do the job just as well, and at less expense than maintaining weather aircraft. The costs involved probably had more to do with it than any improved satellite capability, as only aircraft can record data from inside a storm, and accurately pinpoint the center of one. Nonetheless, on June 30th 1990 the 53rd WRS was deactivated, for the third time in its history. The reserve's 403rd Wing would retain a limited weather recon role with the 815th WS. There would be no aircraft coverage at all of typhoons in the Pacific, which had formerly been the job of the WC-130s of the 54th WRS. Based at Anderson AFB, Guam, the 54th had stood down in September 1988. This unit had the misfortune on October 12, 1974, of losing a WC-130; this has been the only such loss to date. WC-130H 65-0965 was operating over the South China Sea into Typhoon Betsy when it vanished, taking with it all six of its crew.

The folly of relying purely on satellites was demonstrated by several years of intense tropical storm activity that did billions of dollars of damage. Thus, the Hurricane Hunters are still busy, and in November 1992, the 815th was renamed the 53rd WRS, inheriting the former active duty unit's heritage. The composite nature of the parent 403rd was recognized in July 1994, when the "airlift" designation was done away with, reflecting the wing's dual WC-130 weather recon and C-130 transport roles. The 53rd has begun replacing its aging WC-130Hs with seven new WC-130Js.

Airborne Sprayers

Airborne spraying of chemicals understandably got a bad name when it became clear that the Agent Orange defoliant used in Vietnam was responsible for a host of health problems suffered by US veterans and others who were exposed to it. Use

View of the twin Modular Airborne Fire Fighter System dispenser nozzles. C-130s equipped with MAFFS can carry 3,000 gallons of retardant. *Courtesy Paul Hart Collection*

of defoliants as weapons were outlawed by President Gerald Ford, but the former *Ranch Hand* UC-123s were retained in service as pesticide sprayers. These were active against a variety of insect problems at US installations, but by the 1980s were reaching the end of their lives. The obvious replacement was the C-130, and thus Lockheed got a contract to produce sprayer kits for installation aboard C-130s. The modular kits consist of four spray tanks, each with a 500-gallon capacity, plus control equipment. The special equipment can be rapidly offloaded to restore the carrier aircraft to standard airlifter configuration.

The 757th Airlift Squadron "Blue Tigers" of the 910th AW, USAF Reserve at Youngstown, Ohio, flies the spray mission, and has been active in this role worldwide, including missions over Guam, Panama, and Puerto Rico. The C-130s can cover much more territory than the old Providers could, being able to spray a quarter-million acre area in the course of a four-hour flight.

Civilian Herks, notably those of Southern Air Transport, have also seen used as aerial pesticide sprayers; another type of spray mission carried out by the Hercules has been the dropping of dispersents over oil spills in order to lessen environmental damage.

CHAPTER FIVE

USCG and Antarctic C-130s

Coast Guard Herks

Aside from the USAF, the major operator of search and rescue C-130s is the US Coast Guard, which has flown the hercules for nearly forty years. The advent of long-range maritime patrol aircraft during World War II allowed the postwar Coast Guard to supplement its cutter force with air assets for the service's rescue and law enforcement roles. The service placed its first order for the Hercules in 1958, specifying a SAR version of the USAF's C-130B.

The USCG shared the Navy designation system in use at the time, and thus the aircraft were ordered as R8V-1Gs; the "R" being the designator prefix for Lockheed aircraft, and the "G" suffix being used for Coast Guard aircraft. The SC-130B designation was later used, until the "S" prefix for rescue aircraft was replaced by "H."

While the HC-130B would be capable of airlift missions, the primary focus would be on long range search and rescue, with the aircraft being able to search for over seven hours (with two engines feathered to conserve fuel) at low level while 1,000 miles from its home base. Once survivors had been located, rafts and other equipment could be airdropped, and parajumpers could also be sent down to render assistance.

Beyond SAR, Coast Guard Herks have been tasked with such missions as fishery patrol, support of USCG LORAN navigation stations, drug trafficking interdiction, and disaster relief. Some Herks tasked with fishery protection duties have been fitted with FLIR systems for nighttime operations. Another major mission for the Coast Guard's Herks has been protecting shipping in the North Atlantic from icebergs. Since the sinking of the RMS *Titanic* in April 1912, the US has participated in searching for bergs that could endanger shipping lanes, and has been part of the International Ice Patrol since the program's founding. The advent of long-range search aircraft in World War II allowed the IIP to be gradually shifted to an air

The US Coast Guard's Herks are used for a multitude of tasks, from law enforcement to search and rescue. *LMASC*

Coast Guard 1600. USCG Herks fly from both coasts, and on operational SAR missions use the callsign "Rescue" plus their fuselage number. *LMASC*

operation after the war, and the USCG flew C-54s, PB-1Gs/B-17s, P4Y-2G Privateers, and HU-16Es in the IIP role prior to the introduction of the Hercules:

Spotting bergs is done both by visual means and the use of several types of radar, including the APS-137 forward-looking set and the pod-mounted APS-135 side-looking system. IIP missions are staged out of St Johns, Newfoundland.

Starting in the mid-1970s, the Coast Guard began procurement of the HC-130H model to replace its original Herks. These did have the dorsal blisters of the USAF rescue aircraft, and as USCG helicopters have never been fitted for aerial refueling, the tanker pods are not carried. A number of HC-130Es were also operated, but these were later transferred to the USAF for use as C-130H transports. In the early 1980s, the USCG received ten HC-130H-7s; although based on the C-130H airframe, as a cost-saving measure these aircraft were powered by T56A-7 engines removed from their HC-130B predecessors. In July 1997 it was announced that the powerplants of these aircraft would be updated to -15 standard by Allison.

Aside from its standard HC-130s, the Coast Guard also formerly operated EC-130E 1414, which was used to check the LORAN navigation system. This aircraft went into service in 1966, but has since been retired.

The Herk's ruggedness has served the USCG well, as evidenced by the accident suffered by CG 1706 on 24 January 1992. Shortly after departing Dutch Harbor in the Aleutian Islands, the front reduction gearbox and propeller of 1706's number three engine failed, and actually came off the aircraft. The debris punched a large hole in the fuselage, did damage to the tail, and severed hydraulic lines, but the crew managed to put the aircraft safely on the ground at Cold Bay, Alaska.

Antarctic C-130s

US Naval aviation's participation in Antarctic exploration began with Admiral Richard Byrd's overflight of the South Pole in 1929, but the modern age of research dates to 1946 and the USN's *Project High Jump*. In 1955, the Navy prepared to support US scientific operations in the south polar region under *Project Deep Freeze*. For the next forty years, the USN would fly Deep Freeze missions for the National Science Foundation, supporting both US and international research efforts.

Despite the hazards of polar flight operations, use of ski-equipped aircraft would be essential for opening up the continent, and thus in 1955 squadron VX-6 was commissioned at NAS Patuxent River, Maryland. The unit's early equipment included R4Ds, R5Ds, and P2Vs, On December 14, 1955, the first flight to Antarctica from another continent was achieved by VX-6, all previous aircraft either having been shipped in, or in the case of the *High Jump* operation, flown in from aircraft carriers.

The ski-equipped Skymasters and Neptunes were really interim types, as a transport with more capacity was needed. Before the USN could take delivery of its own ski-equipped C-130s, the USAF's 61st TCS deployed its C-130Ds to Antarctica in 1960 to support that season's Deep Freeze effort. Deliveries of C-130BL models for the Navy began in 1960, and these began operations the following year. Later redesignated as LC-130Fs, these C-130B derivatives would form the backbone of the USN's air support on the continent. Aside from transport missions, the aviators of VX-6 would use their Herks for mapping the Antarctic wastes and SAR support of the multinational outposts and teams scattered over the continent.

The "normal" flying season in Antarctica is September through February, during the southern hemisphere's summer. However, it would not be long before an out of season flight had to be made. In April 1961, at a US station in Marie Byrd Land, nearly a thousand miles from McMurdo, Leonid Kuperov,

HC-130H 1710 at RAF Fairford, July 22, 1989. *Robbie Robinson*

HC-130H 1721 taxiing at RAF Lakenheath on September 25, 1988. This aircraft later became the sole EC-130V. *Robbie Robinson*

a Soviet scientist working at the US facility under an exchange program fell ill, and it was decided that his condition was too bad to wait for the summer resumption of flights. As the flying season was over, the C-130BLs were not in Antartica or New Zealand, and one had to be flown with a double crew of 23 from Quonset Point, Rhode Island, to Christchurch, a distance of nearly 10,000 miles. The Hercules departed New Zealand for McMurdo on April 9, and the following day picked up Kuperov and brought him back to McMurdo prior to an evacuation off the continent. In all, the mission covered better than 14,000 miles and demonstrated the Navy's capability to reach Antarctica by air regardless of the season. Perhaps aiming to downplay the US feat, Kuperov claimed several days later that his condition had not warranted evacuation, and that the rescue flight had not been necessary. Another rescue of Soviet personnel occurred during Deep Freeze 87 when the squadron recovered survivors of an I1-14 crash.

The recovery of Kuperov would not be the last wintertime flight made by the LC-130s, as several other medical emergencies would occur that demanded more care than was available on the continent. On June 26, 1964, a VX-6 crew landed at McMurdo to pick up a Seabee that had broken his back in a fall. Not quite two years later, on June 6, 1966, another flight was made to bring back a worker that had sufferred a ruptured bladder.

In the late 1960s and early 1970s, the squadron underwent several changes. The first was the unit's redesignation as an Antarctic Development Squadron (VXE) in 1969. Delivery of seven LC-130Rs (derived from the USAF's C-130H) began in

the early 1970s, and in 1973, the unit moved from Rhode Island to Point Mugu, California.

Just getting to Antarctica can be a challenge. The nearly 2,100 miles between Christchurch and McMurdo means that beyond a certain point, aircraft no longer have the fuel necessary to get back to New Zealand, and are committed to a polar landing. Once in the south polar regions, navigation is both increasingly difficult and absolutely vital, given the harsh conditions and lack of diversionary fields. Even high-frequency radio, the primary means of long-distance communications in the region, is subject to disturbances, and satellite coverage is spotty. Navigation demands constant attention, as there are virtually no navigation aids and standard magnetic compasses are of little use, given the nearness of the pole. Fortunately, during the standard *Deep Freeze* season the sun is always up, allowing sextant shots to guide grid navigation. Operating from unprepared fields holds it own problems, such as getting a heavily loaded Herk airborne from a snowfield. Even when the aircraft are safely on the ground, exceptional care must be taken during maintenance to protect both aircraft and ground crews from the effects of the cold.

The squadron's achievements have not come without cost, and several mishaps have claimed lives and aircraft. On December 4, 1971, LC-130F 148321 was seemingly lost while on a mission to support a team making a cross-country journey to chart ice currents. During takeoff from the D59 site, the crew triggered the JATO bottles, but one broke free and struck the number four engine. The crew managed to crash land the stricken aircraft, and fortunately there were no casualties. The aircraft itself was not a total loss, but the end of the Antarctic summer was looming, and there was little to do but abandon the Herk at D59. Although Antarctica receives very little precipitation, blowing snow eventually covered the aircraft, and by the late 1980s only the top of the tail could be seen.

By all rights, this should have ended the saga of 321. However, while inhospitable in the extreme for human life, Antarctica's cold and lack of precipitation are excellent for preserving machinery. Artifacts from the 1800s still survive intact to the present day, and the various aircraft wrecks that litter the south polar region are protected from corrosion. A survey had revealed that 321's airframe was basically intact despite its icy encasement, and the prospect of recovering the "lost" Herk was appealing to the Navy and NSF, as the surviving LC-130FlR fleet was small and increasingly heavily tasked. The estimated $10 million cost of recovering and rehabilitating 321 was much less than the $38 million it would have cost to build a new LC-130R, so an operation was launched to retrieve the Herk from its icy grave.

On December 9, 1987, mere weeks before 321 was to take to the air once more, LC-130R 159131 was lost in a crash at the site while ferrying in parts for the recovery effort. A fire broke out after the crash, and though workers repairing the other LC-130 managed to rescue nine of the crew, two others died from their injuries. Damage was extensive enough that this latest loss could not be salvaged, so it seems that the D59 site was destined to be the final resting place of a LC-130. To make matters worse, the newly lost aircraft was the only example to be fitted out for photographic mapping.

VXE-6 CO Commander Jack Rector and four others of the squadron were ready to take 321 out on the morning of January 10, 1988. After making one of two planned high-speed taxi tests, Rector lifted off around 6pm and set out on the 800nm flight, accompanied by the "chase" LC-130. Shortly before 11pm, the Herk reached McMurdo and made an uneventful landing at Williams Field.

In January 1975, VXE-6 had the extraordinary bad luck of losing a pair of LC-130s at the same site, within hours of each other. On January 15, aircraft JD319 was detailed to bring back French and Soviet scientists from a site known as *Dome Charlie*, some 600 miles west of McMurdo. The five scientists boarded and the crew attempted to make a JATO takeoff, but one of the rockets blew up, showering the starboard wing with shrapnel. The takeoff was aborted, but with the port engines still running the aircraft did a 180-degree turn before coming to rest. All aboard managed to evacuate safely, but the ensuing fire burned the starboard wing off. Once it was safe to do so, the crew crawled atop the aircraft and released the emergency raft to gain access to the hand-cranked emergency CW transmitter included in the kit. Using this and a HF radio running off a battery, they managed to make contact with sistership JD129, which was then diverted to retrieve them. Three attempted takeoffs from the site could not get JD129 off the ground, and a fourth try resulted in part of the nose gear break-

HC-130H 1718 at RAF Mildenhall, May 27,1995. *Robbie Robinson*

ing off and the Herk coming to a halt. Fortunately, JD131 managed to land and bring all the personnel back to McMurdo. The accidents did cause major problems for the Antarctic support effort into the next season, and subsequent LC-130 flights had to make maximum use of the aircrafts' capabilities to help offset the losses.

Besides the intertheater supply aspect of their mission, the Navy LC-130s also supported a variety of activities within Antarctica itself. These included the dropping of automated solar-powered weather stations throughout the continent, re-supply of the Byrd South Pole Station and other outposts, hauling equipment and construction materials, support of teams transversing the ice, and assisitng with long-duration balloon flights.

The US is not the only nation to use Herks in Antarctica, as New Zealand's No. 40 Squadron also operates C-130Hs on the continent in support of *Operation Ice Cube*. As is the case with the US operations, Christchurch serves as the jumping off point. However, the RNZAF aircraft are not ski-equipped, and thus only operate during the period following the antarctic winter that the blue ice runway on the ice shelf near McMurdo is useable to heavy aircraft. During this "window" the USAF operates C-141Bs and even C-5s onto this runway, allowing heavy and outsized loads to be brought in by air, and permitting the Herks to concentrate on other missions. Brazil has also used C-130s in the Antarctic.

Despite VXE-6's illustrious record, the squadron's history was nearing an end by the mid-1990s, when the drawdown of US forces forced a consolidation of arctic transport units. It was decided that the New York ANG's 109th would be tasked with both the arctic and antarctic missions, gradually taking over from the Navy until VXE-6 was distestablished in March 1999.

Forward attachment mast for a longwire High Frequency antenna on a Coast Guard HC-130H. USCG Herks make use of HF for long-distance communications when on missions. *Chris Reed*

CHAPTER SIX

Reconnaissance and Electronic Warfare Models

The C-130 "Ferrets"

For decades, little has been said publicly about a very "hot" part of the Cold War, namely the undeclared but very real hostilities that took place between Western reconnaissance aircraft and Soviet air defense forces. Apart from the well known CIA U-2 overflights of the USSR, for decades "ferret" aircraft flew along the vast Soviet borders, soaking up electronic emissions of all kinds, while trying to entice Soviet operators to turn on the radars so as to record and analyze their signals. Harassment by MiGs was common, and there were numerous shootdowns.

By the late 1950s, the RB-29 and RB-50 ferrets were reaching the end of their lives; Boeing's RB-47 replaced these aircraft in SAC service, but the USAF also turned to Lockheed and its new transport design. While not having the sheer per-formance of the Stratojet, the C-130 had plenty of room for mission equipment, and as an added bonus, could attempt to pass as a standard transport. A total of eleven C-130As were rebuilt as C-130A-II ferrets under the *Rivet Victor* program for use in Europe, mainly operating from the USAF base at Rhein-Main, West Germany. They were also active from bases further to the south, such as Athens, Greece, and Incirlik, Turkey. One such mission would end in tragedy, throwing a spotlight on what was otherwise a secretive mission.

On September 2, 1958, C-130A-II 56-0528 left Incirlik on its final flight. Aside from the six-man flight crew, eleven mission operators from the Air Force Security Service, assigned to Detachment One of the 6911th Radio Group (Mobile) were onboard. The US would later claim that the aircraft's flight plan was to have taken it first to Trebizond, then to Van, and then

EC-130E ABCCC of TAC's 7th ACCS in the SEA scheme, at Mildenhall on 17 May 1980. *Robbie Robinson*

back to Incirlik, all the time remaining in Turkish airspace to conduct what was termed a study of radio propagation. What actually took place was that the US aircraft strayed across the Turkish border into Soviet Armenia while eavesdropping on Communist communications. Listening posts in Turkey monitored the flight's progress, but were helpless to intervene as four MiG-17s intercepted the ferret and raked it with cannon fire, the burning aircraft impacting some thirty-four miles from the Armenian capitol of Jerevan. Although the US knew that the aircraft had come to a violent end, it initially stated publicly that the aircraft was merely "missing," and the USSR and Iran were even asked for their assistance in finding it. Such "help" was forthcoming, as six days later, the Soviets declared that they had found the remains of the C-130A-II, and had discovered six bodies.

Following the public revelation that the aircraft was down in Soviet territory, there was a good deal of concern that some or all of the eleven missing men were being held captive. This was with good reason, as during several of the 1950s shoot-downs, crewmen were seen escaping from burning aircraft, only never to be heard from again. With the end of the Cold War, reports have come out of the former USSR that some of these men were captured by the Soviets, interrogated, and then lost in the vast Gulag system. Such a fate apparently did not befall the missing members of -0528's crew, as released MiG gun camera footage and eyewitness accounts had no parachutes being seen, and the attack and subsequent crash were judged violent enough to have killed all onboard.

The Soviets accused the US of violating their territory, claiming that the C-130 had flown a considerable distance into

Two views of EC-130E ABCCC, in the new two-tone gray EC-130 scheme. *Courtesy Paul Hart Collection*

their airspace before "falling" to the ground. Quite possibly the US crew were the victims of malicious beaconing or "meaconing" by the Soviets, who intended to lure the aircraft in to create an incident. The recovered bodies were returned later in September, but only four were able to be identified at the time. An ID on one of the unknown bodies was made by modem DNA analysis decades later. A 1993 expedition to the crash site by a US recovery team yielded several thousand bone fragments as well as a piece of the aircraft, and on September 2, 1998, the fragments were buried in a communal grave at Arlington National Cemetery to represent the entire crew.

The end of the Cold War has allowed more details of the various spyplane losses to come to light, and in an effort to publicly honor all the crews that were lost, the National Vigilance park has been created at Fort Meade, Maryland, the home of the National Security Agency. The centerpiece is a C-130A externally reworked to C-130A-II configuration and finished in -0528's markings. The aircraft, which had been in storage in Davis-Monthan AFB for years, was restored at E-Systems, and ferried by the 40th FTS, whose flight experience with their NC-130A ASETS testbed made them the only USAF unit to have current C-130A time. The memorial was dedicated on September 2, 1997.

-0528 remains the only ELINT Hercules known to have been brought down by enemy fire, with the remainder surviving to be reconverted to C-130A transports. Similar to these aircraft were the dozen C-130B-II conversions initially used by the 556th RS at Yokota AB Japan. There were also operations conducted from Cam Ranh Bay, South Vietnam, and the aircraft took over the Rhein-Main mission for a time, starting around 1972. All C-130B-IIs survived to once again become

transports by the mid 1970s. Replacing the older C-130 ELINT aircraft and a small number of Boeing EC-97Gs were three C-130E conversions (62-1819, -1822, and -1828).

Ferrets over the Med

The Soviets were not the only ones to object to being monitored by C-130 ferrets. On March 21, 1973, a C-130 was attacked over the Med by Libyan Air Force fighters. This would be the first in a series of aerial altercations between US aircraft and the forces of Muammar Khaddafy that would continue sporadically into the 1980s. Around noon Libyan time on that day, a C-130 operating from Athens, Greece, was intercepted some 83 miles off the Libyan coast by a pair of Mirages. The fighters signaled by waggling their wings that the C-130 should follow them and land, but the US crew moved toward cloud cover to escape. COMINT operators aboard the C-130 then heard Libyan ground controllers ordering their aircraft to open fire. The Mirages fired approximately 100 cannon rounds, but none hit and no missiles were launched. The fighters again spotted the C-130 a few minutes later, but turned back, presumably due to low fuel.

The Berlin Run

Aside from the peripheral ferret missions, C-130s also conducted missions over Communist East Germany itself. These flights were made possible by the November 1945 agreement with the USSR that gave the US, France, and Britain access to their enclaves in Berlin via three air lanes. The -130s (and other aircraft) could thus gather intelligence on Soviet forces deployed in East Germany, while the US could claim that they were nothing more than transport aircraft. Cover stories

EC-130E *Rivet Rider* 63-7773 of what was then designated the 193rd Electronic Combat Squadron, in June 1981. *Robbie Robinson*

EC-130E 63-7816 of the 193rd Special Operations Squadron.
Courtesy Paul Hart Collection

aside, the Soviets knew what was going on, and during the 1950s there were numerous instances of MiGs harassing and even destroying Western aircraft.

Aside from the ELINT potential of such flights, the US also wanted to demonstrate its right to fly aircraft such as the C-130 into West Berlin. Despite the resolution of the Berlin Blockade, tensions over the divided city remained at a fever pitch well into the 1960s, and another blockade could have been put into place at any time. The original Berlin Airlift had worked, but it had been a back-breaking affair for aircrews, maintenance people, loaders, and air traffic controllers, which had to keep the steady stream of C-47s and C-54s coming and going into Berlin. With the C-130, any future airlift, while still immense, could use fewer aircraft and put less of a strain on crews. The -130's performance could also be used to show the Soviets that the US could and would fly aircraft above the 10,000 foot ceiling that the USSR claimed in the corridors, and which the western powers did not recognize. Until that time, C-119s had been used for the Berlin run, and although an improvement over the C-54s previously used, the "Dollar-Nineteen's" 8,000 foot operating altitude posed no challenge to the Soviet ceiling restriction.

The first flight by a C-130 to West Berlin was staged in late March 1959, and was not without incident. The Soviets were of course aware that such a flight was forthcoming, as the joint US-UK-France-USSR Berlin Air Safety Center had received the flight plans. As scheduled, the flight from Evereaux, France, entered the southernmost corridor, and was soon being buzzed by three Soviet fighters. The harassment continued all the way to West Berlin, with the fighters coming as close as ten feet to the transport. A safe landing was made at Templehof Airport, but the return flight also received an unwelcome "escort" that stayed with them until the C-130 crossed into West German airspace. Not long after this flight, a C-97 flying to

Berlin was also harassed. The US considered sending another C-130 to Berlin in the spring of 1960, but President Eisenhower vetoed this, saying there was no operational need, although he did reserve the right to order such missions if the need warranted. Tensions along the inter-German border remained tense for decades to come, and in 1981 a RAF Berk (believed to be XV192) was damaged by East German gunfire while flying near the border.

The C-130 electronic surveillance mission still exists, as the Pennsylvania ANG's 193rd Special Operations Group flies four EC-130E(CL) *Comfy Levi* aircraft fitted for this role. These aircraft are even more covert than the group's *Commando Solos*, but it is known that they are fitted out for ELINT missions under the *Senior Scout* program, using palletized mission equipment. This can be fitted to other Herks, and has been reported to have been used by other units. The Marine Corps has utilized similar equipment aboard its KC-130s, under the *Senior Warrior* codename.

Tail detail of an WWCTV-configured *Rivet Rider*. Peter E. Davies

Rear detail of a Rivet Rider, showing the fairing behind and above the paratroop door. *Chris Reed*

Open Skies

More than thirty years after the loss of -0528 over Armenia, C-130s were once again flying over the eastern bloc, only this time with the full-knowledge and cooperation of the countries being overflown. First proposed as long ago as 1955 by then-President Eisenhower, the *Open Skies* program was meant to lessen east-west tension by allowing each side to conduct reconnaissance flights over the other's territory.

While the USAF uses the OC-135W in the *Open Skies* role, several countries have flown C-130s on inspection missions. A demonstration flight was made on January 6, 1990, when a Canadian CC-130 set off from the Canadian Forces base at Lahr, West Germany, for a three and a half hour flight over eastern europe. This mission did not carry cameras or other sensors, and was conducted to work up procedures for operational flights.

In early April 1992, a Belgian Air Force Hercules flew over Poland and Belgium with a host of international observers aboard and a Samson pod carried underwing. Produced by Lockheed, Samson takes the place of one of the external fuel tanks, and is controlled via a wireless link with the cockpit. Samson can carry a variety of sensors, including various film-based cameras and the AAS-38 FLIR.

EC-130E Commando Solo

Among the more covert members of the Herk family, the EC-130E *Rivet Rider/Commando Solo* is a psychological warfare platform, equipped for propaganda broadcasting on an enemy's radio and TV channels. Subsidiary missions including acting as an emergency communications station during natural disasters, and providing news and other programming to deployed US forces.

The original *Coronet Solos* were five C-121Cs converted to EC-121S configuration for what was then the 193rd Tactical

Electronic Warfare Group of the Pennsylvania Air National Guard at Middleton, outside of Harrisburg. As the USAF retired its remaining C-121s in the late 1970s, a new platform was needed for the *Coronet Solo* mission, and thus in 1979 EC-130Es were converted from C-130Es by Lockheed Aircraft Services Company. Early reports in the civilian media mistakenly had these aircraft being configured for ELINT missions. They do have some secondary capability in this area, but this mission is primarily carried out by the 193rd's EC-130E *Comfy Levi* aircraft. The program was later known as *Volant Solo* during the unit's period of MAC control; with the transfer of the 193rd to the Air Force Special Operations Command, the mission's codename became *Commando Solo*

The *Coronet Solo IIs* were instantly identifiable by a profusion of aerials, including a large dorsal "fillet" antenna faired into the leading edge of the vertical tail, large underwing "hatchet" antennas outboard of the engines, numerous smaller aerials, ram air intakes for cooling the electronics, and trailing wire antennas for AM-band broadcasting.

Although not used in the tactical transport role, the Rivet Riders retain the C-130E's attachment points for JATO bottles. *Chris Reed*

EC-130E main landing gear fairing detail. *Chris Reed*

The EC-130Es have been active during nearly all of the major US military actions of the post-Vietnam period, starting with the invasion of Grenada in 1983. They also broadcast to the Panamanian population during the 1989 invasion.

During the Gulf War, the *Commando Solos* were pivotal in the propaganda offensive directed against Iraqi forces, working in conjunction with leaflet-dropping MC-130Es. Following *Desert Storm*, a program was launched to upgrade the aircrafts' broadcasting capabilities. As there are different TV formats in use in the Americas and Europe, the aircraft needed to be able to operate on any frequency and format. Upgraded aircraft delivered since July 1992 have four pods containing low frequency TV antennas fitted to the vertical tail, and new underwing antenna pods some six feet in diameter and 23 feet in length. T56A-15 engines and refueling receivers had already been fitted. As the EC-130Es might well be expected to operate over areas were AA threats are present, the aircraft are receiving chaff/flare dispensers to divert missiles, and RHAW gear to warn of radar threats.

The planned invasion of Haiti by the US in September 1994 was scrubbed at the last moment thanks to a diplomatic settlement negotiated by former President Carter and retired Joint Chiefs Chairman General Colin Powell, but the US/UN efforts to keep order among the Haitian military and civilian population, while rebuilding the country meant that the PSYOPS services of the EC-130Es were once again needed. Months before, the Commando Solos had helped stem the tide of Haitian refugees attempting to reach the southern US in makeshift boats by broadcasting in the local language the dangers of making the voyage, and that the US was not accepting such refuegees for asylum.

Among the most actively deployed USAF units, the 193rd was back in action in late 1997, when three aircraft were deployed to Italy. Across the Adriatic in the former Yugoslavia,

Trailing wire antenna pod on the underside of the tail. *Chris Reed*

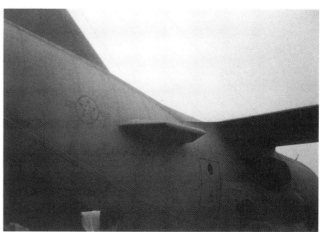

Starboard rear view of an EC-130E, showing the small stencil-type "stars and bars." *Chris Reed*

EC-130E underfuselage antenna detail. *Chris Reed*

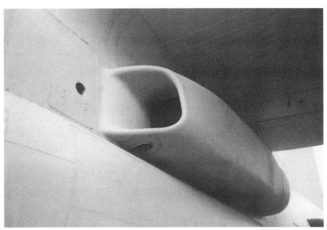

Like other EC-130s, the Rivet Rider's mission equipment generates a good deal of heat; hence the exchanger pods fitted to the sides of the fuselage under the wings. *Chris Reed*

the Serbian Radio and Television network (SRT), under the control of strongman Radovan Karadzic, was stirring up trouble in the still-tense region by airing propaganda broadcasts against Karadzic's opponents and NATO peacekeepers. The *Commando Solos* were deployed to counter this. And in February 1998, an undisclosed number of EC-130Es were deployed to the Persian Gulf region as tensions mounted over Iraqi refusals to allow UN weapons inspections.

Like many of the USAF's special purpose C-130 variants, the *Commando Solo* airframes date from the mid-1960s, and will need replacement not long after the turn of the century. In its FY 1997 budget, the USAF funded the first new *Commando*

Solo aircraft in years, based on the new C-130J. The EC-130J is estimated to have a fly-away cost of $70.5 million apiece.

EC-130E ABCCC

The growing intensity of the airwar in Southeast Asia prompted the US to develop a number of command and control platforms, ranging from the EC-121s to the Navy cruisers and destroyers used in the *Red Crown* radar picket role. However, these were primarily tasked with providing early warning and control for air-to-air engagements; also needed was an aerial command platform for coordinating air to ground missions. Transports had been used as tactical command centers before,

Rear view of an EC-130E, showing the size difference of the fuel tanks between the engines and the larger, braced outboard antenna pods. *Courtesy Paul Hart Collection*

Compass Call **EC-130H 73-390 of the 43rd Electronic Combat Squadron of the 355th Wing at Davis- Monthan AFB, Arizona.** *Robbie Robinson*

but these had been bascially improvised affairs, with plotting boards and radios installed in cabins or cargo bays. The ABCCC program was much more elaborate, centering on the LTV-built USC-15 capsule. Some forty feet long and weighing ten tons, the capsule was designed to fill a C-130's cargo compartment, rolling in and off trailer fashion. The ABCCC aircraft would be able to function as either an extension of a ground station, or as a full-fledged command center.

Nine ABCCC aircraft were converted from fiscal year 1962 C-130E airframes, and for the first decade of service in the new configuration were known as C-130E-IIs.

Exterior modifications included the fitting of ram air inlets on either side of the foward fuselage to cool the electronics, VHF, and UHF antennas under the fuselage, dorsal UHF

Changing a nosewheel on EC-130H 73-1594 of the 43rd ECS.
Peter E. Davies

antennas, longwires running from the,wings to the horizontal stabilizers, and probe antennas under the outer wings. On the interior, there would be sixteen operator consoles, display boards, and extensive radio equipment spanning the HF to UHF bands.

Early on, the ABCCCs were operated by the 314th Troop Carrier Wing, but the 7th ACCS was later formed to carry out this specialized mission. During its years in Southeast Asia, the 7th operated from several different bases. The first movement was to Da Nang, then the unit moved to Thailand, first flying from Korat, and then later Udorn. After the 1973 ceasefire, the 7th was moved the following year to Clark AB, the Phillipines, where it continued to be availible for SEA missions. In the spring of 1975, the 7th coordinated the evacuations of Cambodia and South Vietnam, and the subsequent *Mayaguez* operation. In August 1975 the ABCCC aircraft finally left the area for the US after a decade of operations in the theater. Once stateside, the EC-130Es were based at Keesler AFB, and the 7th became a geographically separated unit of the 552nd AW&CW at Tinker AFB, Oklahoma. The EC-130E designation was adopted around this time. The ABCCC aircraft were later transferred to the 355th Wing at Davis-Monthan AFB, with the 7th ACCS becoming an EC-135 command post unit.

Although updated to ABCCC II standard in the late 1970s, the EC-130E's mission equipment was becoming dated by the mid-1980s, leading to the USC-48 ABCCC III upgrade program undertaken by Unisys. Although the same size as the original capsule, the ABCCC III has far more capability than its predecessors. Paper maps are a thing of the past, replaced by digital imagery generated by a database contained on four 200-megabyte optical disks. These electronic maps can be displayed on the CRTs available at each of the twelve battle staff consoles. As before, the ABCCC III has extensive communications equipment, with three satellite radios being fitted. The mission equipment was designed to be compatible with the JTIDS data link system, allowing fast, secure transfer of information to and from a wide variety of other platforms. This helps alleviate the problems caused by the EC-130's lack of sensors by permitting data from AWACS and other platforms to be displayed.

Using the callsign BOOKSHELF and flying from Aviano, Italy, ABCCC aircraft supported operations over the former Yugoslavia, including the *Deliberate Force* attacks. In this capacity they tied together forward observers and NATO's Combined Air Operations Center, established in April 1993 at Vicenza, Italy.

Three ABCCC aircraft were deployed to NAS Roosevelt Roads, Puerto Rico, in September 1994 to coordinate the invasion of Haiti, which would have included the largest airborne combat drop in fifty years. This task would have been challenging enough, but the last minute diplomatic settlement of the crisis actually created even more work for the mission crews, as they had to improvise plans for an occupation rather than an invasion.

In the spring of 1997, Davis-Monthan deployed an ABCCC to Colorado to coordinate the hunt for a missing A-10, an operation that entailed searching thousands of square miles, using a variety of aircraft ranging from helicopters to U-2s.

Besides the ABCCCs, the USAF has also operated the so-called *Jackpot* aircraft, these being C-130Es with provisions for carrying command modules for coordinating Army ground operations. These aircraft have hookups for additional external antennas to carry out this mission.

EC-130H Compass Call:

As communication and command/control systems have become ever more important in the modern age of warfare, so have the means of destroying, nullifying, or degrading such systems. The "Wild Weasel" SEAD mission and tactical jamming aircraft such as the EA-6B and EF-111A are all part of the equation, but the USAF also operated aircraft equipped with stand-off jamming of enemy C3CM networks. Equipped with the Rivet Fire jamming system, the EC-130H *Compass Calls* were created to counter Soviet and Warsaw Pact networks in the NATO theater. The EC-130Hs were rebuilt from late model C-130Es, and have framework for an antenna array under the tail. There are also blister fairings on the rear fuselage, and air intakes to cool the electronics. The two-tone EC-130 gray scheme is currently applied, and T56A-15 engines have been fitted.

The EC-130Hs originally equipped the 43rd Electronic Combat Squadron of the 66th ECW at Sembach AB in what was then West Germany, but following the lessening of east-west tensions the aircraft were shifted to Davis-Monthan AFB, Arizona, were they became part of the 355th Wing.

The *Compass Call* carries a crew of 13, four of which are the "front end" flight crew. The remainder form the mission

EC-130H 73-1585 of the 43rd ECS/66th ECW at Sembach AB, West Germany in March 1988. *Robbie Robinson*

EC-130H 73-1590, seen in July 1994. *Nick Challoner*

crew, consisting of an Electronic Warfare Officer who also serves as the mission commander, a cryptographer who is also the mission supervisor, a technician to maintain the equipment, and six operators.

Obviously, little is publicly known in the way of specifics in regards to the *Compass Call's* capabilities. It is safe to assume that the jamming suite can operate against either specific networks (even those using frequency hopping) or against a range of frequencies. The *Compass Calls* are primarily tasked with supporting USAF operations, but can also aid other forces, including ground troops. Aside from interfering with voice circuits, the Rivet Fire system can also be used against data links. Missions can be flown against known networks, targets acquired by the aircraft itself, or those detected by other platforms such as RC-135s, EP-3s, and E-3s. In years to come, data may also be relayed from ELINT satellites.

US Navy TACAMO in flight. These aircraft could easily be distinguished from standard Navy transports by the wingtip pods, drogue antenna on the cargo door, and the modified tail. *LMASC*

A pair of EC-130Hs, working with two EF-111A Ravens helped take down Panamanian systems in December 1989. Little more than a year later, Compass Calls were instrumental in countering Iraq's communications nets, effectively cutting off Hussein's forces from each other. EC-130Hs were active against Iraq from both Saudi Arabia and Turkey. By the late 1990s, the Compass Call fleet was to be upgraded to Block 30 configuration with improved mission systems.

Take Charge and Move Out: The Story of the Navy's TACAMO Herks.

By the early 1960s, the US Navy was entering a new era with the entry into service of the first submarines armed with the Lockheed Polaris ballistic missile. Developed under the highest priority, Polaris allowed the Navy to retain a strategic nuclear mission, and gave the US a virtually invulnerable deterrent force that could not be detected and targeted by the Soviets. However, maintaining contact with the new missile subs was difficult, as conventional radio waves do not penetrate water to any appreciable depth. Very Low Frequency transmissions that could reach submerged submarines were the answer, although this meant that data could only be passed at a slow rate. An airborne VLF relay capability was needed, as ground stations would be too vulnerable to attack, leading to the Take Charge And Move Out (TACAMO) program. The VLF band is in the 3-30khz wavelength range, which necessitated extremely long antennas several miles in length, which had to be kept in a nearly vertical position when broadcasting, meaning that the aircraft would have to fly at high bank angles, with weights on the end of the wires.

Early 1960s testing with a converted Marine Hercules tanker and a C-121 proved that the concept was workable; the first production TACAMOs were a quartet of C-130Gs, the first of which was delivered the day after Christmas, 1963. These aircraft, based on the C-130E, had actually been ordered before the 1962 abolishment of the separate Navy designation system, and were to have been designated as GV-2Us. The EC-130G nomenclature was later applied to better reflect the type's electronic mission. Two G-models, 151888 and 151891, became TC-130Gs, the latter aircraft later supporting the *Blue Angels* aerobatic team as its "Fat Albert" transport.

As additional Polaris and later Poseidon boats were commissioned, more TACAMOs were also procured to support them. Eventually, eighteen EC-130Q models were bought, taking over the majority of the mission. There periodic updates to the fleet, such as making the aircraft more survivable to the electromagnetic effects of nuclear deotnations, improved secure communications.

Originally, the TACAMO role was classified, and the aircraft were assigned to fleet support squadrons. VR-1 TACAMOs at Patuxent River, Maryland, supported submarines deployed in the Atlantic, while VR-21 at NAS Barber's Point, Hawaii, supported those in the Pacific. In July 1968, the TACAMO components were orgnaized into squadrons, with VQ-3 at Agana, and VQ-4 at Pax River.

During the more than twenty year history of the TACAMO operation, there were two aircraft lost. The first, EC-130G 151890, was written off after an inflight fire on January 15, 1972. The other TACAMO loss occurred on June 21, 1977, when EC-130Q 156176 of VQ-3 crashed shortly after takeoff from Wake Island, killing all sixteen aboard. The aircraft had

been enroute back to Guam from Hickam AFB, Hawaii, having stopped at Wake to take on fuel. The entire crew was killed.

Beyond the stresses put on the airframes by the requirements of the TACAMO mission, by the mid-1980s the EC-130s were not well-matched to support the *Ohio*-class SSBNs then entering service. Armed with the longer-range Trident SLBM, the *Ohios* could operate over a much wider area than the earlier Poseidon-armed boats, so a new TACAMO with correspondingly greater capabilities was needed. Proposals for improved EC-130s came to naught, and eventually an order was placed for the Boeing E-6A, an adaptation of the E-3 Sentry AWACS. The handwriting was on the wall, but the Herks still had several years of service left. VQ-3 was the first to lose its EC-130s, converting to the E-6Ain 1989. VQ-4 hung onto its Herks until 26 May 1992, with 161531 being the last aircraft to be retired. The new TACAMOs initially used the mission equipment of their predecessors, as this was stripped from the C-130 airframes as they were phased out.

As the era of the TACAMO Herks drew to a close, some of the airframes found other roles, although most would be retired due to their high number of airframe hours. It has been reported that a pair of EC-130Qs took part in Operation *Desert Storm*; but the truth is that these aircraft, 159348 and 159469, were in fact configured as TC-130Qs, and served alongside VR-22's C-130s as logistical transports. To date, the sole TACAMO preserved for display is EC-130Q 161223, at the Marine Corps Air-Ground Museum at Quantico, Virginia.

One EC-130Q has been transferred to the National Center for Atmospheric Research under the civil registration N130AR

EC-130Q 159348 was attached to VQ-4 when it was seen at RAF Alconbury on April 18, 1982. *Robbie Robinson*

RC-130E 2458 of the Forca Aerea Brasileira (Brazilian Air Force). Note the HC-130 type scanning window on the forward fuselage.
Nick Challoner

for atmospheric research work. A variety of sensors can be fitted, including radiometers operating in the shortwave to microwave bands, windsondes and dropsondes, and laser radars for measuring aerosols. There are new optical and sensor ports on the fuselage, and a possible future retrofit program would add a pod housing additional upward-looking viewports atop the foward fuselage. Other EC-130Qs have been transferred to NASA for research work.

EC-130V/NC-130H

A longstanding Lockheed goal has been to produce an AEW/ AWACS version of the C-130 for export. There are many advantages for such a concept, as the Hercules has greater internal volume, range, and endurance than the rival E-2C Hawkeye. An AEW C-130, equipped with the same basic radar as the E-2C, would also be less expensive than the larger and more complex Boeing E-3 Sentry. Coupled with the large numbers of Hercules operators worldwide, this should have ensured brisk sales, but by the late 1990s only one such aircraft has been produced.

By the late 1980s, the US Coast Guard was in need of an AEW aircraft, as it was one of the front agencies for the US government's interdiction efforts against narcotics smuggling from Central and South America. The USCG began flying a pair of E-2Cs in 1987, and subsequently gained several additional aircraft, but was never completely satisfied with the Hawkeye. A longer-ranged type was needed to allow more operational flexibility, as the E-2Cs had to be staged relatively close by their operating areas, providing smuggling rings with warning that they were being watched. The US Customs Service, faced with similiar responsibilities, opted for buying P-3 Orions fitted with AEW radar, but the Coast Guard, with decades of C-130 experience behind it, wanted to convert some of its existing Hercules force to radar platforms. The sole EC-130V was converted from HC-130H 1721, the last of this model bought by the Coast Guard, and fitted with a AN/ APS-145 radar in a Hawkeye-style rotodome. The conversion was carried out by the General Dynamics Fort Worth Division (later to become part of Lockheed), and the aircraft first flew in its new configuration on July 31, 1991.

Budgetary considerations put an end to Coast Guard EC-130V operations in 1993, and 1721 was transferred to the USAF's Edwards AFB and redesignated as a NC-130H avionics testbed, retaining the radome. As of late 1996, this aircraft (re-serialed 87-0157) was still finished in the basic Coast Guard paint scheme.

RC-130A

Most reconnaissance versions of the Hercules have existed in varying degrees of obscurity, but one such model's role was acknowledged. The sixteen RC-130As were built from new for the photo mapping mission, being delivered in 1959. Operated by the 1370th Photo Mapping Group at Turner AFB, Georgia, the RC-130As conducted photographic and geodetic sur-veys worldwide in support of US forces. Photographs could be processed and printed immediately after being exposed, as a darkroom was fitted in the cargo bay. Another sensor, fitted under the nose, was an airborne profile recorder, able to produce exact radar records of terrain profiles. One RC-130A was subsequently rebuilt as a DC-130 drone launcher, and the others were converted back to C-130A transports in the 1970s.

Later, photographic missions were flown by the C-130E *Pacer Coin* aircraft of the Air National Guard's 153rd Airlift Wing "High Rollers" based at Reno, Nevada. One of the *Pacer Coins* was sent to Colorado in the spring of 1997 in order to search for the crash site of a missing A-10, while another was temporarily deployed to Aviano AB, Italy, in September of that year for photo missions over Bosnia. It is also believed that these aircraft also had some degree of ELINT/SIGINT capability. One example is known to have been used as a testbed for electro-optical sensors developed for the Global Hawk UAV.

Overseas Operators

As might be expected, several foreign Hercules operators have used their aircraft in EW /Elint and reconnaissance roles. Israel is known to operate two EC-130Hs; and Egypt also has two EC-130Hs, while Taiwan has one. A pair of Turkish Air Force C-130Bs are also believed to be fitted out for "electric" duties. Morroco uses two H-models (informally designated as "RC-130Hs") fitted with side-looking radar in the port landing gear fairings; in October 1981, prior to taking delivery of these aircraft, the Morrocans lost an ELINT-configured C-130H to a SAM fired by Polisario nationalists. Brazil had three RC-130Es (one being lost in a crash) and at least one of Singapore's Herks may also have a secondary ELINT role.

CHAPTER SEVEN

The C-130H

Despite the introduction of the C-130J, the C-130H re-mains the predominant Hercules model in use worldwide, and thanks to the large number, this is likely to remain so for years to come. Actually, the C-130H designation refers to a whole family of subvariants, all using the T56A-15 engine, but with varying degrees of airframe and system improvements. The line started when the first C-130Hs were delivered to New Zealand in 1965. These were the first aircraft to use the -15 engine, which was uprated to 4,910 shp. Structural limitations dictate a takeoff rating of 4,500 shp, but this is still a significant improvement over the C-130E's T56A-7 powerplants. The first few RNZAF aircraft were basically C-130Es with the new engines, but subsequent H-models have progressively intro-duced new features. Aircraft similiar to the New Zealand Herks were built for export to several countries even before the USAF began placing orders.

HC-130H

The first C-130H variant bought by the USAF was the HC-130H, which was ordered in September 1963. Aside from the Fulton nose and yokes, the HC-130H was easily distinguishable by the large blister atop the forward fuselage, which housed direction finding antennas. The Fulton STAR system as described in the MC-130E section was also fitted, but the HCs had this removed long before the special operations aircraft did, although the Fulton-type nose was retained. Two internal

HC-130H 65-0972 (Lockheed construction number 4121) of the 71st Rescue Squadron/347th Wing at Yokota AB, Japan during 1994. *Takanobu Okamura*

93

One of the first USAF C-130Hs, 74-679 served with the 7th Wing's 40th Airlift Squadron during 1996. The 7th was one of the first active units to receive H-models. *Robbie Robinson*

C-130H in European I colors. *Courtesy Paul Hart Collection*

1,800 gallon fuel tanks could also be carried for long-range missions. Surviving aircraft have been modified with HC-130P type drogue refueling pods underwing.

The first HC-130H flight took place on December 8, 1964, and between 1965 and 1968, 63 were delivered to the Air Rescue Service of MATS/MAC. In Southeast Asia, the HC-130s were known as "Kingships" after their radio callsign of "King," an identifier still in use today. Aside from refueling rescue helicopters, the Herks also functioned as command aircraft, coordinating the often dozens of fighters, tankers, and other support aircraft involved in a single rescue.

Among the record flights achieved by C-130s is the February 20, 1972, mission by a HC-130H crew that set a turbo-prop straight-line distance record of 7,587 nautical miles from Taiwan to Scott AFB, Illinois.

A Plethora of H-Models

The first USAF transport model C-130Hs were bought in Fiscal Year 1973, and were known as "Super Es," as they were again C-130Es with the new -15 engines.

The definitive C-130Hs of later years replaced the gas turbine compressor power unit of earlier C-130s with an APU situated in the lower forward portion of the port landing gear fairing. On the exterior of the fairing, there is a rectangular opening for the inlet, and a circular exhaust above and aft of this. For ground operation the APU provides starting air to the

Based in Alaska, C-130H 74-2131 of the 517th Airlift Squadron/3rd Wing is seen here on a visit to Japan in 1993. *Takanobu Okamura*

C-130H 92-3283 of the 328th AS/914th Airlift Group. *Takanobu Okamura*

powerplants, and electricity from an AC alternator. In flight, the unit cannot be used to supply air, but can continue to furnish electrical power up to a maximum operating altitude of 20,000 feet. As with any turbine engine, ground running of the APU requires crews to stay well clear of the inlet and exhaust, and to check the area for any foreign objects that could be sucked in.

C-130 production from FY1978 onward concentrated on providing aircraft for the USAF Reserve and Air National Guard. Receipt of these new aircraft allowed the reserve com-

C-130H 86-0419, seen at the time on the strength of the 911 Airlift Wing/AFRC at Pittsburgh, sporting nose art. *Chris Reed*

mands to gradually phase out their older C-130A/Bs, which had in turn replaced C-119s and C-123s. The arrival of the C-130 in the reserves helped mark the beginning of the "Total Force" concept, where "second-line" units would be equipped and trained to a similiar standard as their active-duty counterparts. This followed a long period during which the ANG and reserves were equipped with older types with little real combat capability. Far removed from the "weekend warriors" of decades ago, present-day Guard and Reserve C-130 squadrons participate in real-world missions, ranging from disaster relief to airlift operations into Bosnia.

While most of the active-duty composite wings have been broken up, the ANG continues to operate mixed fighter/C-130 units. Herks were first assigned to fighter units in the 1980s to serve as operational support types, being used to transport support personnel, parts, and support equipment.

Among the more unusual missions carried out by Guard C-130s has been the dropping of hay to livestock trapped by snowstorms. Such flights were carried out as early as the late 1940s by C-82s, and half a century later C-130s of the Wyoming ANG were again making such missions, each dropping thousands of pounds of baled hay to cattle in New Mexico.

The Kentucky Air National Guard's 123rd Airlift Wing at Louisville received the 2,000th Hercules on May 16, 1992, as the unit began a transition from its C-130Bs to newer H-models. The aircraft in question, 91-1231, was the first aircraft to be equipped from the outset with the Lockheed SATIN self defense system. Missile warning sensors are located on the tail and nose, with dispensers under the tail, to either side of the nosegear, on the fuselage above the main gear fairings, and on the pylons. IRCM transmitters can also be fitted on the aft part of the gear fairings. Manual control of the countermeasures is the responsibility of the navigator, whose station has several new control panels and a pistol grip for triggering the dispensers. While the self-defense system is a valuable means of protecting transport flying into high threat areas, it is not without its hazards, for example the IRCM units present an optical danger within a certain radius, and pylon-launched flares could potentially hit the aircraft's flaps if these are extended too far.

The modern US military's emphasis on fighting at night led to late model C-130Hs being fitted with lighting compatible with night vision goggles; this includes the cockpit instrumentation, cabin, and exterior lighting. Refitting earlier aircraft to this standard is a priority for the ANG, to ensure that these aircraft remain fully mission capable. Another new item is the Secure Communications and Navigation System, using a ring laser gyro and GPS.

The Guard and Reserve H-models are to remain in service for some time to come, and it is possible by the time that they are due for retirement an entirely new tactical airlifter design will finally be on hand to replace the Hercules. However, it is perhaps equally likely that a further extrapolation of the basic C-130 design will meet that need instead. The Herk still has room for growth, and it is possible that a "21st Century C-130" with J-model engines and system, a more voluminous fuselage, and other improvements may yet take to the air.

A smaller number of C-130Hs have been provided to frontline units, principally at Dyess and Little Rock, with the 50th Airlift Squadron "Red Devils" at the latter base being the first to receive the C-130H3 model.

Warning receivers and missile approach sensors in the modified "beavertail" of 90-1794. *Chris Reed*

Troop Transport

The ground troop capacity of standard C-130Hs is 78, with seats (each with a 20-inch separation) being placed in a double row in the center of the cargo compartment, and single rows on the sides of the compartment. Seating for an additional fourteen is possible when the wheel well walls are equipped with seats.

Airborne missions allow for 64 troops to be carried, with seat spacing increased to two feet. Prior to the drop, the crew brings the aircraft to a speed not exceeding 150kts, extends the airstream deflectors, and opens the paratroop doors. The troops are cued by the red (CAUTION) and green (JUMP) lights on the doors, which are controlled by the pilots. Retrieval of static

Although without engines or a vertical tail, this Hercules hulk continued to serve with the 911th AW as a ground trainer. *Chris Reed*

Later C-130s such as 90-1794 of the 179th Airlift Wing do not have provisions for JATO. *Chris Reed*

Italian C-130, seen on a mission supporting the *Frecce Tricolor* **Aerobatic Team.** *Courtesy Paul Hart Collection*

lines is taken care of by two winches.

Congo/Zaire

Since the 1960s, C-130s have periodically seen action in the Congo, a former Belgian colony of strategic importance due to large deposits of important resources such as copper and other metals. The Congo descended into turmoil nearly as soon as it became independent in 1960, leading to UN military intervention. Trouble again flared in 1964 when rebel Simbas began attacking government forces; in response the US deployed C-130s to the Congo to provide support for mercenaries fighting the Simbas for the Congo government. The rebels began

seizing western hostages in August, subjecting them to brutal treatment and torture.

After several months of fruitless attempts to diplomatically free the hostages, by November the time had come for a rescue mission, to be carried out jointly by US and Belgian forces. Operation *Dragon Rouge* ("Red Dragon") got underway when C-130s on TDY to France embarked Belgian Red Beret paratroopers and flew to Ascension Island, subsequently deploying to the Congo itself to await the final order. The operation went forward on the morning of November 23rd, with the paratroopers seizing the airport at Stanleyville, allowing subsequent aircraft to land there. The hostages were quickly

C-130H MM61998 of the Italian Air Force. *Peter E. Davies*

freed, although some were massacred just before they could be rescued.

Nearly a decade and a half after *Dragon Rouge*, the siutation in the area was little better. Six years after the country was renamed Zaire in 1971, there was an invasion by Katanga rebels operating from Angola; this was repulsed, but the following year the rebels again attacked, this time seizing the city of Kolweizi. Following the capture, some Europeans living in the city were killed and others held hostage. Fear of more atrocities, as well as Soviet influence on the Katangas, caused western countries to edge closer to intervention. The Zairean Army staged an airdrop on May 16, but this went badly, with the majority of the paratroopers being quickly dispatched by the Katangas. This cinched western involvement, and within several days the French Foreign Legion's *2nd Regiment Entrangere Parachutiste* had been deployed to the Zairean capitol of Kinshasha. On May 19 the 2nd REP dropped on Kolwezi with four C-130s and a single C-160 Transall. Plans had called for an additional aircraft of each type to participate in the operation, but these were not availible, so the C-130s carried more paratroopers than the standard load of 64. The French troops quickly secured the city, and Belgian paratroopers brought in by C-130s helped in the evacuation of foreigners. The RAF also deployed a number of Herks to Zaire with field hospital equipment. USAF participation in the operations included strategic airlift with 18 C-141s and a single C-5A.

Almost twenty years after the 1978 rescue mission, Herks were once again in the Congo, which had since reverted to its original name. In June 1997, as violence once again wracked the country, two MC-130Hs of the 352nd SOG were forward deployed to Germany on June 9. The next day, one of the aircraft flew to the capitol of Brazzaville to deliver a special operations team to survey the situation and assess any threat to the US Embassy, as well as pick up any Americans trying to leave the country. Despite fighting close to Brazzaville's airport, the crew managed to land successfully, deploy the team, and take on 56 Americans and foreign nationals in just over twenty minutes. In all, the mission lasted 21 hours, requiring three heavyweight inflight refuelings by Mildenhall-based tankers. The aircraft returned to pick up the team on June 18.

Entebbe

It was perhaps inevitable that the Israeli Air Force would come to operate the Hercules, once the US became the primary supplier of combat aircraft to Israel in the late 1960s. The first Herks arrived in 1971 and have subsequently participated in many operations, but the most illustrious by far has been the July 3-4, 1976, mission to free Israeli and other hostages from Entebbe, Uganda. The Entebbe Crisis began on June 27, 1976, when an Air France Airbus was seized by four terrorists, who forced the crew to fly to Entebbe, Uganda. Once there, the highjackers demanded that Israel free imprisoned terrorists; it soon became apparent that Ugandan President Idi Amin's regime was giving support to the highjackers, who eventually released many of the hostages but kept 105 of Israeli citizenship or Jewish heritage.

Further angered by such blatant action, the Israeli government nonetheless had little immediate choice but to try negotiations, while preparations for a rescue mission proceeded at breakneck speed. The only aircraft capable of taking rescue teams to Uganda was the C-130, although even the Hercules did not have the range to make the round trip; a refueing stop

One of the survivors of the 1983 Falklands War, C-130H 16805 is on the strength of Argentina's 501 Esq. *Peter Davies*

C-130H B-680 of the Danish Air Force's Esk721. *Peter E. Davies*

somewhere in Africa would be mandatory on the way back.

Following a full-scale demonstration assault, the rescue plan went forward, and four Herks were launched. Accompanying the C-130s were two Israeli Air Force Boeing 707s; one was configured as an airborne command post and relay platform that would circle Entebbe as the raid was underway. The other was fitted as a flying hospital and would wait in Kenya, a nation with whom Israel still enjoyed good relations. Despite being unescorted for the majority of the flight, the Israeli aircraft proceeded unmolested.

The first C-130 touched down at 2301, its approach having gone undetected by means of flying close behind a British cargo flight landing at Entebbe. Having made it to the airport without being seen, the Herk crew taxied their aircraft to a dimly-lit portion of the field. The ramp was lowered, and the assault team, led by Lt. Colonel Yonatan Netanyahu, drove toward the old terminal building where the hostages were being held. In a bit of psychological warfare, the team drove in a black Mercedes and a pair of land rovers, mimicking Amin's own official car and escort vehicles.

Within a few minutes of the first C-130 landing, the other three aircraft also touched down, carrying teams to carry out the operation's other objectives. Israeli planners recognized the possibility that Amin's air force could send MiG-17 and MiG-

C-130H CH-11 of the Belgian Air Force. These aircraft are being refitted for service well into the 21st Century. *Nick Challoner*

Turkey has been a long-time user of the Hercules, taking delivery of five C-130Es in 1964. More than three decades later, aircraft 186 of No.222 Squadron flies on, one of the few military Herks in a natural metal finish. *Peter E. Davies*

21 interceptors after the departing C-130s; fortunately, the Ugandan MiGs were based at Entebbe, and a group was detailed to destroy them on the gound.

Once the hostages had been freed, a final group of commandos took them to the waiting C-130s. The aircraft would have to be refueled to make it back to Israel, but rather than do so at Entebbe it was decided to wait until the force was on the ground at Narobi. Less than an hour after the assault began, aircraft carrying the hostages departed. Three hostages had been killed, along with Netanyahu; 35 Ugandan soldiers and 13 terrorists had died. After taking on fuel at Nairobi and transferring the wounded to the waiting 707, the force was homeward bound by the early morning hours of July 4.

The Stretched Models

Although the US military has not thus far been a major customer for the stretched C-130H-30 series, a number of overseas air arms have procured H-30s or the commercial L-100-30 equivalent. These have included Thailand, Malaysia, Egypt, Kuwait, South Korea, Thailand, and the United Arab Emirates. Most of these operators bought their aircraft new, but Portugal initiated a rebuild program for their existing C-130Hs, and by 1997 a pair had been stretched to H-30 configuration.

For many years, the French Armee de L'Air was one of the few western european air forces not to operate the C-130, preferring instead to standardize on the smaller European-built C.160 Transall. However, the Herk's capabilities finally won French orders, and a trio of standard C-130Hs was delivered in 1987, followed in 1988-90 by nine H-30s.

In 1987, a C-130H-30 achieved several airdrop records during a presentation to the US military at Fort Bragg. Up to that point, the world record for a single pass CDS drop was 16 bundles, but the Super Hercules dropped 24 (with a total weight of 43,262 lbs) in three seconds. Another world record was achieved by dropping a field artillery section (eight paratroopers, one pallet with ammunition, another with a M102 howitzer, and another with a utility vehicle) in a single pass. And finally, the drop of 92 paratroopers set a US record.

International Incidents

On April 2, 1976, a Royal Saudi Air Force C-130 on a routine run from Damascus, Syria, to Riyadh, Saudi Arabia, experienced navigational problems and crossed into Israeli territory near the border with Lebanon. Israeli fighters were scrambled and intercepted the transport; at the time memories were still fresh of a 1973 incident where a lost Libyan airliner had refused to follow Israeli aircraft and had then been shot down over the Sinai. Fortunately, the Saudi aircraft followed the interceptors and was led to a landing at Ben-Gurion Airport in Tel Aviv. A total of 36 people were on board, mostly soldiers, but including three American civilian personnel serving as part of the flight crew. The following day, the aircraft and its crew were released to continue their interrupted journey to Riyadh.

The Hercules was in the news again in August 1988, when a C-130 was involved in the death of a head of state. On 17 August, Pakistani President General Mohammad Zia ul-Haq had just departed Bahawlpur when the C-130 he was flying on exploded and crashed, killing all aboard, including the presi-

C-130H 545 of the Israeli Air Force's 103 Squadron. *Robbie Robinson*

84001/841 of the Swedish Air Force's F7 unit. Local designation for the Hercules is Tp84. *Neil Dunridge*

C-130H 844, also of F7. Despite Sweden's neutrality, its Herks have seen overseas use in a number of humanitarian operations. *Nick Challoner*

dent, senior Pakistani military leaders, US Embassador Arnold Raphael, and senior US defense attache General Herbert Wassom. The group had flown to Bahawlpur to witness a demonstration of the US M1 main battle tank.

Within hours of the crash, allegations began to spread that Zia's C-130 had fallen victim to a shoulder-fired SAM, a bomb, or other sabotage, Zia having had a number of enemies that could have orchestrated such an attack. On October 13, it was disclosed that an American crash investigation team, consisting of USAF and Lockheed personnel, believed that a missile or bomb was not responsible for the crash. Although the aircraft had been reduced to small pieces, the wreckage had fallen into a more or less a confined area, and there was no evidence of a high-order explosion. Nonetheless, three days later, a Pakistani report was issued that pointed toward some type of sabotage.

Sometimes, incidents can occur even between countries that are ostensibly friendly to each other. One such case, involving a C-130, took place in April 1992 over Peru. A major focus of US C-130 operations in the Southern Command region has been drug interdiction, including reconnaissance flights to locate processing facilities and airstrips. Codenamed *Furitive Bear*, such flights over Peru especially targeted the Upper Huallaga Valley, a major coca-producing region.

The Furitive Bear flights were coordinated with Peru, and at least on paper were allowed to overfly the country. However, a power grab by Peruvian president Alberto Fujimori in April 1992 led to a cooling of relations between the two coun-

The Swedes fly some C-130 relief missions under the auspices of the United Nations, hence the all-white UN scheme on this C-130H. *Anders Edback*

Aircraft 847 of the Swedish Air Force braking heavily upon landing. *Anders Edback*

View of 847 undergoing maintenance, with the T56 engines partially uncovered. *Anders Edback*

tries, and soon US military crews flying over the region were on alert, as the Peruvian air force began aggressive patrolling.

Tensions finally erupted when a C-130H of the 310th AS, operating from Howard AFB, Panama, set out over the valley. Reports of an unidentified aircraft over the region, combined with communications mishaps and the general air of hostility, led the Peruvians to scramble Su-22 *Fitter* fighter-bombers, which easily overtook the converted transport.

The Peruvian fighters attempted to force the US aircraft to follow them, but the C-130 crew continued to run for international airspace. The Su-22s followed the C-130 for hundreds of miles, until the transport was over the Pacific some sixty miles off the Peruvian coast. This should have put the American aircraft safely over international waters, but Peru claimed a 200-mile limit that the US did not recognize. Final-

ly, the *Fitters* opened up with their cannon, aiming for the US aircraft's cargo door. The door was blown open, and MSgt Joseph Beard was sucked out of the aircraft, and two others onboard were injured. Despite a subsequent search, Beard's body was never found. Having already taken damage and one fatality, the crew had little choice but to put the stricken Hercules down at a Peruvian airfield near the border with Ecuador.

In the fall of 1997, during one of the periodic flareups in tension between Turkey and Greece over the island of Cyprus, a Greek Hercules carrying that country's defense minister on a trip to the island was reportedly intercepted and buzzed by Turkish F-16s. More than two decades earlier, following the 1974 Turkish-Greek clash over Cyprus, US C-130s had brought in humanitarian aid to victims of the hostilities between the two NATO allies.

Aircraft 842, in a slightly different Swedish scheme, with larger national insignia and the lettering even with, rather than below, the cockpit. *Anders Edback*

Swedish Herk 844 displaying markings for Sarajevo airlift missions in 1994. The blue sack marks the 100th mission, while the boxes with red crosses designate medical supply flights. *Anders Edback*

Interior view of the cargo compartment of a Swedish C-130. *Anders Edback*

Desert Shield/Desert Storm

Iraq's invasion of Kuwait on August 2, 1990, and the resulting US deployment to protect Saudi Arabia and the other Gulf states meant that American Herks would once again be flying into hostile skies. In many cases, MAC units were flying the very same C-130Es that had seen action in Vietnam more than twenty years previously, but there were to be major differences between the war now brewing in the gulf and the previous onflict in Southeast Asia.

The Kuwaiti Air Force had been a Hercules operator since the early 1970s, when two L-100-20s had been delivered. One was written off and the other sold, but these were replaced by a quartet of larger L-100-30s. During the invasion, one of the Kuwaiti Herks was destroyed on the ground, but the remaining aircraft made it safely out of the country, joining KAF A-4s and Mirages for what turned out to be a months-long exile across the border in Saudi Arabia.

Iraq had nearly taken delivery of C-130s itself, as during the 1980s the US Commerce Department announced that an export liscense for six L-100s to Saddam Hussein's regime would be approved. This sale was never acted upon, and Iraq's air force continued to rely upon Soviet-built An-12 *Cub* and IL-76 *Candid* transports.

While the huge *Desert Shield* strategic airlift effort got most of the public attention, a large proportion of the USAF's C-130 fleet was at least as busy in a tactical role, taking supplies and equipment from the main airfields to forward locations.

The US Marine Corps also deployed its KC-130s to the gulf, with the tankers taking up station at Muharraq, Bahrain, to provide refueling support to the FA-18s and AV-8Bs stationed in the area. The Corps is reported to have equipped one or more of its KC-130Ts in the theater with the *Senior Warrior* ELINT system.

As a substantial percentage of the USAF's Herk force was preoccupied with gulf-related duties, provisions had to be made to maintain other operations. Southern Air Transport L-100s carried out some US missions, while German C-160 Transalls took over from rotational Herks normally based at RAF Mildenhall in the UK.

C-130s ranged throughout the gulf region, with bases of MAC's 16th Air Division (Provisional) including Bateen, Ail Ain in the UAE, Masirah, off Oman, Sharjah in the UAE, and Thumrait. the provisional units included both active duty C-130E/Hs and aircraft from the USAF Reserve and Air National Guard that had been participating since the beginning of the crisis. Additionally, B- and E-model Herks from Mildenhall were present at Incirlik AB, Turkey, to support activities there.

Swedish AF loadmaster Anders Edback using a remote-controlled winch to prevent a maintenance container from falling from the edge of the ramp while being unloaded. *Anders Edback*

The cramped cargo compartment of aircraft 844 loaded with two maintenance containers and loading equipment on the ramp. *Anders Edback*

With the expansion of coalition forces in preparation for an offensive, RAF Hercules C.1s also began flying intratheater transport missions, with deployed aircraft being based at King Khalid International Airport in Riyadh. Like the USAF's Herks, the RAF's C.1s spent a good deal of time operating from desert strips, and coatings were applied to protect fuselage undersides from damage. By the start of *Desert Storm*, seven aircraft were on hand, supplemented by a pair of C-130Hs from the Royal New Zealand Air Force sent over in late December. Whereas the USAF kept virtually all of its aircraft in their standard colors, the RAF repainted many of its tactical types in "desert pink" schemes, and this extended to at least one C-130. The RAF was also stretched thin, and Spanish C-130s took over some British missions in Europe.

The Saudi capitol's airport also hosted the French C-130Hs of ET61. Other nations that contributed C-130s to the gulf effort were Australia, with C-130Es from No 37 Squadron, and South Korea, with a C-130H. The coalition's Arab partners also contributed Herks, including Saudi Arabia and the United Arab Emirates.

As the tense standoff turned to war in January 1991, the deployed Herks were absolutely essential in the preparations for, and execution of, Desert Sabre, the 100-hour ground war against Iraq. While the world's attention was focused on the coalition's air offensive, C-130s moved Army forces from staging areas to forward bases on the western border of Saudi Arabia and Iraq, in preparation for the "Hail Mary" offensive from this unexpected quarter. Once the attack began in late February, Herks helped sustain the fast-moving mechanized and air- mobile forces as they plunged deep into Iraq. The transport crews also prepared to act in the medevac role, taking

casualities out of desert strips near the front lines to rear areas for treatment.

Despite the Coalition victory, there would be little rest for C-130 crews, for as in addtion to moving men and material back from the field for return to the US and Europe, a new situation developed in Northern Iraq. Encouraged by the US, Iraqi Kurds had taken up arms against Hussein's regime, only to be savagely put down when American help did not materialize. Attempting to flee from Iraqi forces, thousands of Kurds were soon trapped in mountainous regions in the Turkey/Iraq/Iran border region with little or no means of keeping themselves alive. Faced with a humanitarian disaster, the US belatedly came to the Kurd's rescue, launching *Operation Provide Comfort to* get supplies to the refugees via C-130 airdrops and helicopter missions, and eventually setting up safe havens in northern Iraq.

American C-130s have been common visitors to the Gulf region in the post Desert Storm years, supporting the continuing military presence in Kuwait, Saudi Arabia, and elsewhere. Herks have also supported the periodic larger-scale deployments of troops and aircraft countering Iraqi saber-rattling. Airlifters have also been used in such contingencies as the mass relocation of US units following the Khobar Towers terrorist bombing.

On August 7, 1998, following the terrorist bombing of the US Embassy at Nairobi, Kenya, the 4404th Wing (Provisional) flew a C-130 mission to the Kenyan capitol to deliver a medical team and supplies; the following day another flight brought in body bags for those killed in the explosion.

New Commands, New Units

In the massive reorganization of the USAF that took place after Desert Storm and the end of the Cold War, there were significant changes in the organization of the C-130 force. A new concept was the creation of composite units combining tactical and transport aircraft within a single wing. One such composite unit was the 23rd Wing at Pope AFB, tasked with both delivering Army forces into battle and providing close air support. The 23rd had C-130Es for transport, with F-16s and A/OA-10s for tactical missions. The unit was the successor to the 23rd Fighter Group and the American Volunteer Group "Flying Tigers" of World War II, and painted its C-130s with the famous "sharkmouth" markings.

The melding of such diverse types of aircraft in a single wing was not entirely successful; on March 23, 1994, a F-16D collided with a C-130E in the landing pattern at Pope; the Hercules, although damaged, managed to land, but the fighter's crew ejected and the Falcon struck an area where Army paratroopers were preparing to board a C-141B, killing twenty-four. The 23rd's F-16s were later transferred to Canon AFB to replace retiring F-111 Aardvarks.

On April 1, 1997, the USAF's C-130 fleet underwent yet another change of command, with most of the Herks formerly belonging to Air Combat Command being returned to Air Mobility Command, where they had been up to 1993. The 23rd Wing was further split up, with the unit's C-130Es now coming under the 43rd Airlift Wing, and the A-10s making up the 23rd Fighter Wing. The distinctive "sharkmouths" on the former 23rd Herks were gradually painted out as the aircraft underwent maintenance. Likewise, the 7th Wing at Dyess AFB, Texas, was split up, with its C-130s going to the 34th AW and its B-1Bs going to the 7th Bomb Wing.

For the most part, the USAF's C-130 fleet continued to wear the SEA camofluage for years after the war in Vietnam, but during the 1980s, the European 1 "lizard" scheme was introduced. Following *Desert Storm*, the European 1 scheme was gradually replaced on USAF airlifters by an overall flat gray

Interior view of paratroop door. *Chris Reed*

scheme. The single coat of paint used has proven easier to maintain and weighs less than the two-coat camouflage did.

Currently, training for USAF Herk crews is provided by the Air Education Training Command's 314th Airlift Wing at Little Rock AFB, Arkansas. The 314th was an Air Combat Command unit until April 1997, and two of the wing's four squadrons, the 50th and 61st Airlift Squadrons, retain an operational transport role. Training is done by the 53rd and 62nd ASs, both flying C-130Es.

Somalia

In the last weeks of his presidency, George Bush announced that the US would take part in *Operation Restore Hope*, an international effort to maintain order in war-torn Somalia to permit delivery of relief supplies, and to help rebuild the country's infrastructure.

Somalia was not exactly an unknown for C-130 crews, as since the summer of 1992, both active duty and ANG aircraft had been flying in relief supplies as part of *Operation Provide Relief*, based out of Mombasa, Kenya. Prior to this, Italian Herks had brought out refugees fleeing the country, while Libyan L-

Maintenance container being loaded. *Anders Edback*

Hercules of the United Arab Emirates, in another variation of desert camo. *Nick Challoner*

100s and C-130s transported arms and material to Somalian factions supported by Colonel Khadafy.

One of the difficulties faced during *Restore Hope* was that only the airport in the capitol city of Mogadishu was able to take large transports, and even there conditions were bad. C-130s took the material out into the Somalian countryside, operating into austere strips. Aside from those belonging to the USAF, Herks from the RAF, Italy, and Saudi Arabia were also active in Somalia.

Provide Promise

American military airlifters have been flying mercy missions since before the USAF was a separate service, but few have been as long-term as the 1990s relief efforts into the former Yugoslavia. When Yugoslavia broke up, ancient tensions between the component republics flared into civil war, resulting in a level of conflict and atrocity not seen in Europe since World War II. While western powers were wary of becoming militarily ensnared, the plight of civilians in the state of Bosnia-Hercegovina finally spurred action. Following its declaration of independence, the republic had been under attack by Serbian nationalists who encircled the capitol of Sarajevo. The former Olympic city was being torn apart by the bombardment, its hundreds of thousands of citizens shot at, shelled, and starved. Ground supply convoys were stymied by the Balkan terrain, roadblocks, and outright opposition by various factions. An airlift operation would avoid many of these problems, at the expense of sending transport crews into hostile airspace, heading for fields with few or no navigational aids which were subject to shelling and sniping. Despite these hazards, the situation was so desperate by the summer of 1992 that the United Nations authorized additional peacekeeping forces and a hu-

manitarian airlift, operating from Sarajevo's airport, which was to be turned over to UN jurisdiction by the Bosnian Serbs. Termed *Operation Provide Promise* by the US and the British, the UN flights would also involve Hercules flights by Canada, France, Italy, and Sweden, as well as C-160 Transall missions from Germany. Austria would also contribute by opening its airspace to military flights, thus cutting down on the flight time to and from Germany.

Control of the Butmir Airport passed from Serbian troops to the UN in late June, but securing the facility had to wait for the overland arrival of a Canadian armored battalion. The first USAFE operations began on July 3, when C-130s left Germany, laden with rations and forklifts to aid in offloading other aircraft at Sarajevo.

A narrow corridor was established through which the transports were supposed to be safe from AAA and SAMs; such assurances from the warring parties were of little comfort to the airlift crews. Missiles in use by the combatants ranged from shoulder-fired SA-7s to SA-2s and SA-6s. As much flight time as possible was spent over the Adriatic before making the inbound leg.

Coming into Sarajevo was even more hazardous, necessitating assault-type landings. Once on the ground, unloading began rapidly, as despite the UN control of the airfield, firings and mortar shellings were all too common. Frequent sniping at aircraft taking off and landings led to crash programs to fit C-130s and other transports with cockpit armor. Crews also wore flak jackets as an extra measure of protection. Firings on transports would often lead to temporary halts to the airlift; one such attack took place on April 10, 1995, when a 37th Airlift Squadron Herk was hit a dozen times by small arms fire, fortunately without injury to the crew.

The only fixed-wing transport lost during the Bosnian operation was an Italian Air Force G.222 that was shot down by a SA-7 SAM approximately 20 miles west of Sarajevo on September 3, 1993. A pair of US Marine Corps CH-53Ds with AH-1 escorts attempted to reach the crash site, but were unable to stay long due to enemy fire. All four crewmen aboard the G.222 were killed.

The hazards of Bosnian flying spurred efforts to fit C-130s and other transports with defenses and countermeasures. The shoulder-launched SAM threat to transports had been around since the later stages of Vietnam, but little had been done to provide airlifters with any means of protection. USAF C-130s flying over Bosnia received the *Snowstorm* self defense system. Another refit program added ALQ-131 jamming pods to at least 29 C-130s; the -131 had been previously used on EC-130Hs as a self-defense measure. Bosnian operations have also spurred many other C-130 operators to refit their fleets; New Zealand, for example, under *Project Delphi*, has contracted with Raytheon E-Systems to put in cockpit armor, chaff/flare dispensers, and warning receivers.

Despite the airlift, many civilians in outlying areas were still starving, as by early 1993 Serbian forces were able to block most roads in eastern Bosnia, keeping aid convoys from getting through. On February 25, President Clinton announced that the US would soon begin airdrops over Bosnia. In order to keep the C-130s out of the range of ground fire, the missions would be flown at 10,000 feet, which would seriously impair the accuracy of the drops. It was acknowledged from the start that some of the material would end up in Serbian hands, but this was unavoidable, and airdrops would at least give some relief to the surrounded Bosnian enclaves.

Before the operation could begin, Serbian, Croatian, and Bosnian representatives had to inspect the crates at Rhein-Mein to ensure that no arms or other military equipment were being dropped. Leaflets were also dropped over the targeted areas; beyond letting the civilians know that aid was on the way, it was also hoped that the warning would keep people from entering the drop zones prematurely and being crushed by the falling containers.

The first missions took place early on March 1, with three C-130s dropping 22 tons of supplies and returning to Germany without taking any hostile fire. As predicted, the accuracy of the high-altitude drops left something to be desired, with recon satellite imagery showing that most of the pallets had missed the intended drop zone.

Despite initial skepticism of airdrop operations by some European allies, French and German C-160 Transalls were later brought in, flying joint missions with the larger American C-130s. There would be 2,220 US airdrop missions, with the majority of these being Container Delivery System drops.

The history of the Bosnian war is full of atrocities and an appalling loss of civilian life; one mortar strike alone on a Sarajevo market on February 5, 1994, killed 68; some of the hundreds injured were flown out of Bosnia by a quartet of USAF C-130s for medical attention in Germany.

Bevy of Canadian Forces Herks in a variety of paint schemes. *LMASC*

C-130H 7004 of the Royal New Zealand Air Force. *Nick Challoner*

Continued bombardment of cities, failed cease-fires, firings on UN personnel and aircraft, and the general deepening of the war prompted the NATO *Operation Deliberate Force* in late August 1995. Unlike earlier piecemeal strikes that had to go through the UN for approval, the *Deliberate Force* attacks had the desired effect, bringing the warring factions to peace talks at Dayton, Ohio.

The signing of the Dayton peace accords between the warring factions in Paris in late 1995 reopened long-closed overland supply routes, and spelled the end for *Provide Promise*. The last missions were flown in to Sarajevo on 9 January 1996, with a 37th Airlift Squadron C-130E being followed by a French Hercules. In two and a half years, USAF aircraft had flown 4,597 sorties; when combined with RAF, French, arid Canadian C-130 flights

Herk 996 of the Fuerza Aerea De Chile. *Nick Challoner*

and German C.160 operations, the sortie number climbed to just under 12,900, with over 160,500 met-ric tons being delivered.

The end of *Provide Promise* in no way marked the departure of C-130s from the Yugoslavian skies. As part of the accords, a western Implementation Force (IFOR) would be deployed to help in the transition, keeping the peace and monitoring compliance. This called for major deployments of troops and materials; some of this could be brought in by road, but a substantial airlift operation was also put into place. The region was broken up into sectors, with the US contingent working out of the former MiG base at Tuzla. To keep the former warring parties in line, NATO units were given broader rules of engagement, allowing commanders to react quickly to potential threats. The first *Joint Endeavour* mission landed at Tuzla in December 1995, and by April 27 of the following year one thousand such flights had been made. A C-130H of the 39th Airlift Squadron of the 7th Wing carried out the 2,000th mission on October 21, 1996.

The *Joint Endeavour* mission ended a year after it began, but the problem of restoring a lasting peace to the region was proving to be a long term one, and the western military mission was to be continued under the name *Joint Guard*, with IFOR being renamed the Stabilization Force (SFOR).

Haiti

The invasion of Panama in 1989 showed that the paratrooper still had a place in modern warfare, and in the fall of 1994 an even larger airborne operation was in the offing. The Caribbean island of Haiti, under the control of a military junta headed by General Raoul Cedras, had become a humanitarian nightmare, with rampant abuse by the military and police. With conditions on the island deteriorating and many Haitians attempting to flee to the US aboard homemade rafts, contingency plans to seize Haiti and restore President Jean-Bertrand Aristide went ahead.

Markings worn by a C-130H of the 911th Airlift Group commemorating its placing in the 1989 Volant Rodeo airlift competition. *Chris Reed*

Natural metal H-30 making a vehicle airdrop. *LMASC*

As last-minute negotiations were underway on September 18, the US military enacted a plan designed to take Haiti by force. *Operation Restore Democracy* would have included the largest airborne combat operation since World War II, involving 61 C-130s and other transports. On the afternoon of the 18th, paratroopers from the 82nd Airborne Division were brought to Pope AFB, where they enplaned for the trip south; Herks were also launched from MacDill AFB, Florida. AWADS-equipped E-models from Pope would serve as pathfinders, while 28 C-130Hs from Dyess AFB carried heavy equipment and vehicles, including nine ancient M551 Sheridans, the only air-droppable tanks in the US inventory.

The airdrop was to have taken place at 12:01am on the 19th, with nearly two thousand paratroopers being dropped around the Haitian capitol of Port-au-Prince and the nearby airport. The initial drop would be supplemented by an airmobile assault by 82nd Airborne UH-60s operating from the island of Great Inaugua and follow-on drops by C-141Bs; altogether nearly 4,000 paratroopers would have been dropped. Had the invasion gone ahead as planned, ANG and USAF Reserve C-130s operating from Dobins AFB, Georgia, would have carried combat engineering teams to Port-Au-Prince to repair any damage incurred to the runways there, allowing heavy transports to land.

The possibility of Cuban MiG-21s or -23s getting close to US transports was to be avoided at all costs, and so F-15s were deployed to Roosevelt Roads NAS, Puerto Rico, to maintain patrols between Haiti and Cuban bases. Cuban fighters were briefly in the air during the operation, but came nowhere

Herk G-273 of 334th Squadron, Royal Netherlands Air Force. *Robbie Robinson*

C-130H-30 16806 of the Force Aerea Portuguesa, seen in 1995. *Peter E. Davies*

As demonstrated at Edwards AFB, the C-130H-30 can drop an entire field artillery section in one pass. *LMASC*

near US aircraft. Aside from the fighter cover, and AC-130 fire support, A-10s from Shaw AFB were also on hand to suppress threats with their 30-mm cannon.

Nearly four hours before the drop time, the C-130s received a recall order—negotiations between former US President Carter, retired General Colin Powell, and Haitian junta having resulted in a peaceful end to the junta's rule and Aristide's return. The forcible invasion was canceled, being replaced by a US-led peacekeeping mission, *Operation Uphold Democracy.*

Assured Lift

The conflict in Rwanda spurred Operation Support Hope in July 1994, with USAF C-130s bringing in relief supplies to refugees fleeing from Rwanda into neighboring countries. And, in November-December 1996 a pair of Herks flew missions in peacekeeping operations in Rwanda, *Operation Guardian Assistance.*

Following the end of the brutal civil war in Liberia, the US assisted in peacekeeping operations by helping move in troops from neighboring African nations. The 86th at Ramstein was again in the forefront, conducting flights into Liberia from Cote D'Ivoire, Ghana, and Mali.

In Unfriendly Hands

While the C-130 has been exported to US allies worldwide, there are several C-130 customers whom the US would now prefer not to be equipped with the type. For example, Libya ordered a total of sixteen C-130Hs between 1968 and 1970 before the US-Libyan relationship deteriorated. Libya paid in full, and the first eight aircraft were delivered, but the sup-

port the Khadafy regime gave to international terrorists led to the State Department cutting off arms sales to Libya. Libya attempted to get the other eight by various means, but they remained in storage at Marietta. A 1979 Libyan order for a dozen L-100-30 commercial versions of the C-130 was also turned down, although a number of commercial Herks did end up in Libyan service. There were reports that Libya was to take delivery from Vietnam of former South Vietnamese Air Force C-130As captured in 1975, but this did not go through. At least some of Libya's Herks were fitted out by the early 1990s as probe/drogue refueling tankers to support long-range missions by Su-24 *Fencers.*

Iran is another formerly friendly nation that operates the C-130. Fueled by his immense oil wealth, Shah Rezah Pahlavi spent enormous amounts of money on US-made weapons in the 1960s and 1970s, especially on aircraft. In all, Iran bought 21 C-130Es and 43 C-130Hs, and would have certainly bought more had Pahlavi not left the country in 1979 for exile, and eventually death. Like Iran's other US-made aircraft, their C-130 force suffered after the cutoff of spare parts, and perhaps a dozen are currently in operation, no doubt using parts cannibalized from other aircraft. On October 4, 1982, an Iranian Hercules on a domestic flight was highjacked by several non-commissioned officers seeking asylum in the US or elsewhere. Most of the hostages were set free during a stop at Dubai, in the United Arab emirates, but the highjackers were denied refuge there, and at Sharja, also a part of the Emirates. After being refused permission to fly into Lebanon, the C-130 was taken back to Iran, landing at the airfield at Bandar Abbas, where the highjackers were imprisoned.

Stretched -30 model of the Royal Thai Air Force, in commercial-type colors. *Takanobu Okamura*

An Iranian Herk was again in the news on March 17, 1994, when an aircraft on a diplomatic flight from Moscow went down near the capitol of embattled Nagarno-Karabakh. The crash killed all 13 crewmembers and 19 passengers, principally family members of the staff at Iran's Moscow Embassy, returning to Tehran. There were allegations that either Armenian or Azeri forces fighting in the region had destroyed the C-130, as well as charges that the aircraft had been on a spy flight, which was denied by Iran.

CHAPTER EIGHT

The Future Hercules

For the most part, the story of the C-130's technical development has been one of steady improvements rather than radical leaps. From the original YC-130 to the C-130H3s of the mid-1990s, the basic airframe/powerplant combination remained essentially the same, with the C-130J being the first standard transport model to depart from this formula. Several times during the production run proposals have been made for advanced derivatives, some of them extremely different from the basic design.

In 1959, early on in the C-130's career, plans were underway for an enlarged model, designated the GL-207 Super Hercules. With a wingspan of 145 feet and a fuselage stretched to 121 feet, the GL-207 would have replaced the standard T56 engines with four Allison T61/550-B7s each rated at 5,000 shp. Payload capacity would have been boosted to 75,000 lb. Several air freight carriers placed orders for GL-207s, but problems with the T61 kept the aircraft from ever leaving the drawing board. The concept for a larger Hercules did not die with this project and helped form the basis for Lockheed's C-141A Starlifter, which although powered by turbofan engines mounted under swept wings had a fuselage cross section identical to the C-130.

During the 1960s, there was a considerable amount of tension between the Army, which was perfecting the concept of airmobility, and the USAF, which was unwilling to let the Army operate the large fixed-wing transports it wanted. Attempting to mollify the Army, the Air Force investigated procurement of a C-130J model, a completely different aircraft from the later model that would bear the same designation. Intended to improve the C-130's already impressive short field performance, the C-130J would have had numerous improvements, including T56-A-15 engines from the HC-130H model. Larger main gear pods would have been added to accommodate an articulated main landing gear capable of withstanding sink

rates of 17 fps at a gross weight of 135,000 lb. The main gear tread would be increased to 20 ft., and larger 56*30-15 tires with 603 square inches of contact would replace the 56*20-20 tires of older models.

Alterations to the control surfaces would have included installation of a trailing edge flap, an increased range of movement for the elevator, and extending the area of the rudder chord by some 40%, and that of the ailerons by 30%. The original C-130J was never to leave the drawing board, but the T56-A-15 was used by the C-130H.

Around the same time the first C-130J was on the boards Lockheed was also planning an amphibious version of the C-130 for the US military to replace such types as the HU-16 Albatross. Costs associated with the Vietnam War kept the program from going into production, but by 1970 plans were underway for a derived commercial version that would serve as a short-haul commuterliner that could operate independently of increasingly crowded airports.

Fitting out the Hercules for water operations would have entailed a fiberglass flying boat hull fitted to the underside of the fuselage with outboard floats under the wings. Landing gear for conventional operations would be fitted, as would a retractable hydroski to buffer the shock of water takeoffs and landings, thus dispensing with the need for heavy reinforcement of the boat hull. The standard T56 engines would be retained, but to maintain inlet clearance, it was planned to use nacelles of the type seen on the L.188 Electra and P-3 Orion with high-mounted intakes. The vertical tail would be enlarged to give more rudder area and extensions to the horizontal stabilizers would be fitted. There would also be a large fillet extension to the vertical tail reaching forward to above the wing.

Despite the advantages of such an aircraft, orders were not immediately forthcoming and Lockheed could not afford to embark on a demonstrator program unaided. Thus, the Amphibious Hercules got no further than a ¹⁄₁₆-scale radio controlled model, but the basic concept was to resurface nearly three decades later.

The C-130 was to reign supreme as the USAF's tactical airlifter through the 1960s and early 1970s, but in 1972, the Advanced Medium STOL Transport program was initiated to replace the Hercules with an entirely new type. Since the C-130's first flight high efficiency turbofan engines had appeared and matured, and much research had been done into STOL operations. Boeing's YC-14 AMST competitor had Upper Surface Blowing, with the exhaust from a pair of F103 engines being routed over the flaps, providing a large amount of lift. McDonnell Douglas' YC-15, which had a fuselage cross section similar to the company's DC-10 widebody airliner, used externally-blown flaps to achieve STOL performance.

Despite their successful test flights neither AMST design won production orders, as the program fell victim to the post-Vietnam defense drawdown and was canceled on February 2, 1978. The need for a new airlifter did not disappear, and Lockheed proposed several Hercules-based derivatives to fulfill at least part of the AMST mission while retaining some commonality with the existing USAF C-130 force.

The Wide Body STOL variant would have increased the C-130's capability to haul outsized items by using a larger fuselage with a cargo hold 11.3 ft. high, 11.7 ft. wide, and 48 ft. long. STOL provisions included horizontal stabilizer extensions, a wide-chord rudder, and reinforced landing gear. The powerplants would have been standard T56-A-15s, but they would have driven new propellers.

The Volume Load Stability version would have retained the standard fuselage cross section, but would have been longer, with a "T" tail and new Allison 501-M-71 engines each rated at 5,600 shp. Significant improvements in payload, speed, and range were predicted. The advantages offered by the WBS and VLS proposals notwithstanding, neither was to receive production orders, as the USAF continued to buy standard C-130Hs.

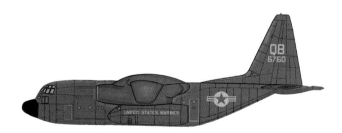

NA-382 in hypothetical USMC colors. *Chris Reed*

During the same time frame the AMST program was running, the US Navy was considering a radical shift to V/STOL types that could operate from smaller, less expensive aircraft

carriers. The service got as far as ordering two examples of Rockwell's XFV-12, a technology demonstrator using augmentor flaps to achieve V/STOL performance. It was realized a V/STOL combat force would need supporting transport/tankers of similar capability, so Rockwell proposed the NA-382, a C-130 derivative using the same augmentor flap technology. One of the most radical C-130 variants ever devised, the NA-382 would have had an entirely new 120 ft. span wing with four General Electric F101-GE-100 turbofans fitted with modified afterburners. For V/STOL operations, ducting in the wing would have fed the engine efflux to front and rear augmentor flaps on each wing. Entraining the colder air flowing across the upper surface of the wing, this would provide more than sufficient lift for VTOL. When closed, the augmentor flaps would form the upper surface of the supercritical wing, being raised halfway for STOL operations and all the way up for VTOL. Ducting would also be run to nozzles in the tail for pitch control in vertical flight.

Projected performance figures for the NA-382 were impressive: in VTOL mode 15,000 lb. could be carried for 800 nautical miles and 5,000 lb. could be carried over 1,600 nm. With a 300 ft. takeoff run 37,000 lb. could be carried for 800 nm and 10,000 lb. for four times that distance. Configured with KC-130 tanker equipment, the NA-382 could take off in 700 ft., fly 2,600 nautical miles, transfer 2,425 gallons of fuel, and return to a 200 ft. landing.

Rockwell planned to build a pair of NA-382 prototypes using government supplied C-130 airframes, followed by an initial production batch of a dozen machines. The aircraft would never leave the drawing board, as the augmentor flap scheme did not work with the XFV-12, which never flew. Conventional combat aircraft would continue to be built so there was no need for turning the Hercules into a "jump jet."

Not all new ideas for the C-130 line would have involved new airframes. In the early 1980s, with fuel prices rising, an Air National Guard C-130 was fitted with twin ventral fins underneath the tail in an attempt to reduce fuel burn by cutting down on drag. The seven foot long, twenty inch high fins could have been refitted to existing aircraft.

The C-130 was even considered in the late 1980s as a potential carrier aircraft for air launched cruise missiles (ALCMs). During this period a number of alternatives to traditional penetrating bombers were being considered following President Carter's decision to cancel the B-1A. Lockheed designed a modular launcher that would fit either the Boeing AGM-86 or the General Dynamics AGM-109 Tomahawk derivative; the primary intent was to use this system to arm new-build C-5s as standoff weapons carriers. The launchers were designed to be compatible with other aircraft, including the C-130, although much more serious consideration was given to larger, longer range aircraft, such as the Galaxy, Boeing 707, YC-14, and YC-15 as ALCM carriers. Such plans never came to fruition, as the USAF opted to fit ALCMs to B-52s and to buy the new B-1B.

The ECX-130 was a 1980 proposal by Lockheed for a new TACAMO aircraft for the USN, in competition with Boeing's 707-derived E-6A. To meet the requirements of supporting the new Trident SSBN force, the ECX-130 would have been extensively revised, nearly to the point of becoming an entirely new design. A stretched fuselage some 119 ft. long would have allowed 60% more payload, but the alterations did not stop there. The entire wing structure would have been replaced with a supercritical wing with two GE/Snecma CFM56 high-bypass turbofans on pylons, with a third engine in the new "T" tail. Wingspan would be increased to 161 ft. and height to 38 ft. The ECX-130's performance would be enhanced, with a top speed of 366 knots and a range of 4,760 nautical miles. Weight was to be in the 250,000 lb. range. Lockheed proposed building a total of forty-five aircraft for service starting in the latter half of the 1980s. Aside from the ECX-130, the company also proposed a less radical derivative based on the existing EC-130Q with improved systems and uprated T56/M71 engines. A plan was offered to build a dozen new airframes and refit ten existing Q models for a total program price of $820 million.

The EC-130ARE Airborne Radar Extension was an early 1980s attempt at marketing the Hercules as an airborne early warning platform. This would have had an APS-125 radar, the same as that carried by contemporary versions of the E-2C Hawkeye, but this would have been fitted in a 24 ft. rotodome atop a shortened vertical tail, thus alleviating the problem of fuselage interference. The basic EC-130ARE configuration would have been a "bare bones" system, with the aircraft set up to relay the radar data to ground stations. The aircraft could also be outfitted for more autonomous operations with three systems operators. In 1981, the state department cleared Lockheed to release data on the EC-130ARE to potential overseas customers. No sales were ever made, and subsequent plans for AEW derivatives have centered on more capable versions with full systems crews and conventional rotodome placement.

There were also several stillborn civilian Hercules developments. The L-400 Twin Hercules was a short-lived 1980 project for a model powered by two 4,900 shp 501-D22F engines, with the wingspan shortened to 125 ft. 8.5 in. The L-400 would have had maximum structural commonality with the C-130/L-100, using the same fuselage and outer wing structure. Changes would have included two-wheel main landing gear, a new center wing section, wingtips, and 14 ft. Hamilton Standard propellers. With a two-man cockpit and reduced fuel consumption, operating costs for the L-400 were projected to be lower, a fact that Lockheed hoped would attract freight haulers that did not need a full-sized Hercules. It was estimated that a worldwide market existed for around 400 aircraft, and deliveries could begin in early 1983. No orders were ever placed.

Likewise canceled were Lockheed's plans for larger L-100 derivatives optimized for taking cargo to and from major freight hubs, serving as feeders for widebody freighter operations. The -40 model would have been stretched twenty-five feet, while the L-100-50 would have a twenty-foot plug forward of the wing and a 16 ft. 7 in. one aft, stretching the cargo compartment to 77.3 ft. and the overall length to 133 ft. Cargo capacity would be nine pallets and a ramp container, or up to 60,185 lb. of other payload. On the exterior, Starlifter-type landing gear fairings would be added to house new articulated gear. The -50 would have been the first Hercules since the first few C-130Es to have a fuselage cargo door. Measuring 114 ft. 108 in., it would be on the forward port side of the fuselage. Derived from the -50 but even larger was the proposed L-100-60, which could have eleven standard sized pallets. These models were to initially use Allison 501-D22E powerplants, but the T56-M71 5,895 shp engine then under development could also have been fitted.

Assault C-130 and Wide-Body Section C-130

In 1984, Lockheed proposed a new C-130 family to meet future airlift needs. The first variant, the Assault C-130, was optimized for combat operations in denied territory, while the Wide-Body Section C-130 would have a larger fuselage cross section to carry bulky loads. Both models would have a number of advanced features in common. The powerplant configuration would be one of them, with four General Electric GE34 turboprops replacing the T56s. The new engine was a derivative of GE's well-proven TF34 low-bypass turbofan and would have been fitted with Hamilton Standard four-bladed contra-rotating propellers. Although heavier than the T56, the GE34 would be considerably more powerful, with a baseline rating of 8,800 shp. Upgrades could have boosted the rating to as high as 11,000 shp, making such an engine more than twice as powerful as the T56A-15.

As with earlier proposals, both variants would have had extensions to the horizontal and vertical tails, as well as increased chord rudders. The wing would have fast acting double-slotted flaps, modified leading edge surfaces, spoilers, and underwing side force generators outboard of the engines.

The WBS' fuselage would have a cargo compartment 140.4 in. wide and 135.6 in. high This increase in size would permit larger cargoes to be carried, such as UH-60s and 155 mm howitzers. Bradley fighting vehicles could also be carried and airdropped. Total payload capacity would be 65,000 lb., and with the new engines and STOL features the WBS could operate from 3,000 ft. airstrips. The Assault C-130 would retain the standard C-130 fuselage, but would have superior short field performance, being able to operate with 44,000 lb. payloads into and out of 1,500 ft. strips.

C-130J

After more than forty years and over 2,000 aircraft produced, the C-130/T56 airframe/engine combination finally ended its production run in 1996. Its successor, the C-130J, originated from a late-1980s program to replace the active duty C-130Es.

A major driving force in the program was the desire to reduce operating costs, made possible by a two-man flight crew and more fuel efficient engines. Lockheed built on their L-100-20 HTTB experience in designing the C-130J, and early plans had the J model being fitted with the same T56 Series Four engines refitted to the HTTB, but the new Allison AE2100D3 engine was chosen instead. The 2100 is a two-spool turboprop using a core derived from the T406 engine of the V-22 Osprey driving six-bladed Dowty propellers. Rated at 6,000 shp (nearly twice the rating of the original YC-130's T56-A-1s), the new engines give the C-130J increased range (2,200 miles with a 40,000 lb. payload), a shorter takeoff run, a faster rate of climb, and higher cruise altitude (29,000 ft). The 2100D3/propeller installation was air tested on a bailed RAF Hercules C-1 (XV181) by replacing the number two T56. The refit was carried out by Marshalls of Cambridge, and flight tests were carried out between March and June 1994.

Internally, the C-130J has a digital flight control system and a glass cockpit with four main screens, five smaller LCD panels, and a pair of HUDs for the pilot and copilot. This constitutes the standard flight deck crew, although a flight engineer

Central to the C-130J's enhanced performance is the Rolls-Royce AE 2100 engine, driving six-bladed Dowty propellers. *Chris Reed*

AE 2100 underside detail. *Chris Reed*

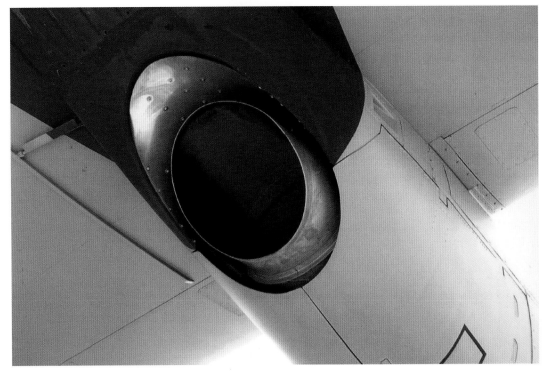

AE 2100 exhaust detail. *Chris Reed*

and navigator can be accommodated if mission requirements dictate. The cockpit instrumentation is fully night vision capable, as is the exterior lighting. Early C-130J plans called for the installation of the APS-133 radar as fitted to the KC-130T, but the Westinghouse APN-241 low power color radar has been fitted instead, giving basic C-130Js all-weather capabilities.

The pylon-mounted fuel tanks are not used, but there are hardpoints on the wings should such an installation be needed in the future. A boom refueling receptacle is an option. Another option is the SKE 2000 station keeping system.

Like late-model C-130Hs, the C-130J is equipped from the factory with provisions for self defense systems. The basic configuration includes the AN/ALQ-157 infrared jammer, AN/ALE-47 chaff/flare dispensers, AN/AAR-47 to detect approaching missiles, and the AN/ALR-56M radar warning receiver. Variations are likely as sales to foreign operators continue. For example, Australian C-130J-30s are to be fitted with a variant of the Project Echidna electronic warfare system, a self protection suite being developed for tactical and transport aircraft.

Originally, the first C-130J flight was to have taken place in fall 1995, but problems with the flight control software delayed this until 4 June 1996. By far the most numerous of the J models, the stretched C-130J-30 was also the first to take to the air. The Royal Air Force has twenty-five (designated Hercules C.4) on order to replace its C.1s; these aircraft are being built with refueling probes fitted atop the left side of the cockpit. The sale of C-130Js to the UK was quite controversial; British Aerospace was totally against such a purchase, as the firm was one of the partners in the European Future Large Aircraft program, which was later to become the A400M. An outgrowth of the earlier FIMA project, the A400M is now a competitor to the C-130J in the international marketplace for C-130E/H and C-160 replacements. In many respects resembling a larger Hercules save for a T-tail, the FLA was designed with higher volume cargo in mind, having a cabin 12 ft. 7.5 in. high, 13 ft. 1.5 in. wide, and 56 ft. 7 in. long. This is sufficient to carry such cargo as medium helicopters or the larger 96*125 in. 3610 pallets. Alternatively, up to 126 paratroopers could be carried. Tanker transport and pure tanker versions were also proposed.

Despite being proposed as early as 1989, the FLA remained very much a paper project into the late 1990s, and could not possibly have entered RAF service until well past the year 2000. Existing C-130s with minimal upgrades were not judged to meet the RAF's requirements, while the much superior C-130J could be put into service relatively quickly. Other factors that helped the US aircraft were the RAF's existing C-130 infrastructure, and the fact that other UK firms were subcontractors for the Lockheed program.

The development of the C-130J was not without troubles. One of these was a change in the stall characteristics due to the new engine/propeller combination. This necessitated the installation of a stick pusher to lower the aircraft's nose in a stall situation; a stall warning system using audio tones and HUD cues is also fitted. Tail fin icing problems were also encountered. Deliveries to the RAF were to begin in 1996, but delays pushed this back to fall 1998.

Although early procurement of J models for the USAF centered on special purpose models to replace platforms that dated to the 1960s, receipt of transport models has since allowed aging E-model transports to be finally retired. To date, two USAF J models have been lost during operations in Afghanistan. In May 2013, C-130J-30 04-3144 went off

The pod underneath the tail for a trailing wire antenna. *Chris Reed*

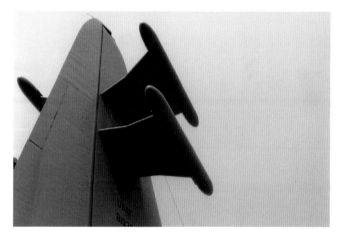

Perhaps most immediately distinctive of the Commando Solo's many antennas are the quartet mounted on the vertical tail. *Chris Reed*

The nose gear, with flare dispensers aft. *Chris Reed*

The aft end of the sponson, with chaff and flare dispensers forward, and the AN/ALQ-157 jamming system occupying space that would have been used for JATO mounting points in earlier models. *Chris Reed*

In common with other "electric" Herks, the Commando Solo sports large heat exchangers to cool the extensive electronics suite. *Chris Reed*

The large pod outboard of the engines and "hatchet" type antenna is not for fuel, but an aerodynamic covering for yet more antennas. *Chris Reed*

Antenna pod mounting detail. *Chris Reed*

the end of the runway at FOB Shank and was wrecked, although the crew safely escaped the burning aircraft. After being stripped of sensitive gear the ruined airframe was demolished. A C-130J from Dyess AFB attached to the 774th Expeditionary Airlift Squadron crashed while taking off from Jalalabad, Afghanistan, in October 2015. The entire six-man crew perished, as did five civilian passengers and three Afghan personnel on the ground.

HC-130J (USAF) and MC-130J

The HC-130J Combat King II, first flown in July 2010, replaces the elderly HC-130N/P; like the earlier aircraft, it is equipped with refueling pods and extensive missions avionics and countermeasures to fly long range combat SAR missions behind enemy lines. The similar MC-130J Commando II can also be tasked with SAR, but is primarily aimed at providing infiltration/exfiltration for special operations forces, replacing the surviving MC-130 Combat Talons and MC-130P Combat Shadows. The first MC-130J deliveries to Cannon AFB took place in 2011.

KC-130J and Harvest Hawk

Now having replaced the KC-130F/R, the KC-130J tanker transport equips two front liner and one reserve Marine Corps squadrons. The J model has a substantially wider envelope for refueling receiver aircraft and can offload more fuel. VMGR-252 was the first operational unit, and in early 2005 took the new Hercules model to war, deploying to Al Asad, Iraq. KC-130Js have subsequently deployed to Afghanistan, Djibouti, Cyprus, and Pakistan.

There was long-standing interest in procuring a kit that could turn KC-130s into a simple gunship configuration with a 30 mm cannon, but this concept matured into giving the Hercules a precision guided munition capability, with a four-round launcher underwing for AGM-114P Hellfire IIs and the capability to drop the AGM-176 Griffon from the cargo ramp or aft paratroop door. To spot targets, an AAQ-30 electro-optical system is fitted in an underwing pod with two fire control officers "running the show" from a pallet-mounted console.

USCG HC-130J

Authorization for an initial six HC-130Js for the US Coast Guard was given in 2001 and these began arriving in 2003, although they were initially used as transports pending the installation of sensors and other mission equipment. Twelve HC-130Js have been delivered or ordered, with an ultimate goal of fielding twenty-two aircraft to replace HC-130Hs.

AC-130J

The AC-130J Ghostrider program is aimed at providing replacements for aging AC-130Us and the now-retired AC-130Hs, converting sixteen MC-130J airframes to gunships. Although much of the AC-130J configuration stems from the MC-130W/AC-130W—with 30 mm Bushmaster cannon and AGM-176 Griffon missiles—starting with the third aircraft, the 105 mm howitzer is to be reintroduced, and plans call for later aircraft to be fitted with laser weapons. The first AC-130J flight took place in late January 2014; the protoype AC-130J (09-5710) was written off after being overstressed during an April 2015 test mission from Eglin AFB.

EC-130J Commando Solo III

After considering the use of used DC-10s as replacements for the long-serving PSYOP EC-130Es, the USAF opted for the C-130J to form the basis for the next Commando Solo variant; by 2006, the EC-130J had completely replaced the older models.

WC-130J Weatherbird

The 53rd WRS operates ten WC-130J Weatherbirds, the first being delivered in October 1999. These replaced the WC-130Hs, and are distinguishable from their J model transport counterparts by the fitting of external tanks to increase endurance during storm recon missions. The Weatherbirds did not reach initial operational capability until 2005, as an extensive suite of meteorological sensors had to be fitted to the airframes.

Further J Model Development

In 1996, an AEW/AWACS version of the C-130J-30 was announced. This would have been equipped with an APS-145 radar and associated rotodome, up to nine operator stations, ESM, data links, and other new avionics and sensors. Australia was targeted as a potential customer, as by 1997–98, the RAAF was actively looking for an AWACS type to fill the Wedgetail command/control role. Competitive aircraft include the Boeing

737-700 with a Northrop Grumman radar and the Airbus A310 with an Elta radar. Although equipped with a basically older radar (although in its latest Group II+ version) and slower and smaller than its competitors, the C-130J did have some advantages over the other types, namely much greater rough field capability, a combat proven airframe and radar, and a high degree of compatibility with the RAAF C-130 transport force. The RAAF chose the Boeing airframe for purchase as the E-7A, and other potential customers including South Korea and Turkey have followed suit.

In fall 2015, Lockheed Martin resurrected the idea of a maritime patrol Herk, this time aimed at providing the RAF with an MPA capability absent since the retirement of the Nimrod force years earlier. The SC-130J program would involve rebuilding the RAF's standard length J models with operator positions, an AESA radar, EO/IR sensors, and underwing weapons pylons.

Rebuild Programs

Although all new C-130s will be J models, earlier variants will be flying in military and civilian colors well into the future. Rebuild programs to keep these aircraft viable are inevitable, and in the late 1990s, Snow Aviation International announced a proposal to bring C-130s up to C-130J standard, with additional improvements. Aside from the installation of new engines and propellers, the C-130M Hercules Plus would also have had a glass cockpit, streamlined wing/fuselage fairings, and wingtip fuel tanks to replace the pylon-mounted tanks. Provisions would be fitted for taking on fuel from drogue and boom-equipped tankers. The C-130M would be available in two stretched versions: the first would have a single four foot plug ahead of the wing, while the second would be stretched twelve feet by fore and aft plugs. No full-up C-130M ever flew, but the company did rebuild WC-130E 61-2365 (N307SA) with eight-bladed props, wingtip tanks, and new electronics.

CHAPTER NINE

The Commercial Hercules

Although conceived of as a military type, the Hercules was always recognized as having considerable potential as a commercial freighter, as its tactical capabilities and features also lent themselves to all manner of civilian freight-hauling, establishing the L-100/L-382 Hercules as the true successor of the DC-3/C-47. Lockheed attempted at first to sell a commercial version of the C-130B, in anticipation of an exponential increase in commercial airfreight traffic by the early 1960s. This version was never built, but on April 21, 1964 the company did fly the Model 382-44K-20, the prototype for the L-100 line. Based on the C-130E, the L-100 (Model 382B) was certified in February 1965, and a total of twenty-two were built. Domestic operators included Alaska Airlines, Continental Air Services, Delta Airlines, and Pacific West; overseas customers included Pakistan International Airlines and Zambia Air Cargo. Surviving L-100s were later rebuilt to stretched configuration, and by the 1990s only one original model remained, in service with the Pakistani Air Force. However, unstretched former military C-130s now being operated commercially are sometimes generically referred to as L-100s. Lockheed next proposed the L-100-10 model, combining the standard L-100 airframe with Allison 501-D22A engines each rated at 4,500shp. This went nowhere, but the new engines would be fitted to the L-100-20 (Model 382E), the first of the stretched Herks. A recurring problem in Hercules operations over the decades has been carrying volume-intensive cargo; nothing short of a major redesign could be done about the fuselage cross section, but it did turn out to be possible to increase the volume capacity by lengthening the fuselage. The L-100-20 had a five-foot plug inserted forward of the wings and a 3 foot 4-inch one aft, thus increasing the cargo compartment floor length to 49.3 feet and the useable volume to 5,307 cubic feet. It proved possible to refit earlier aircraft to this standard (indeed, the first L-100-20 was the reworked L-100 prototype) and some L-100s were

Rolls-Royce RB.211 turbofan engine being unloaded from an L-100-30. Saturn used its L-100s to take RB.211s from the UK to the US for installation on Lockheed L-1011s. *LMASC*

SAT operates worldwide; N918SJ (Lockheed construction number 4208) is seen here at Yokota, Japan in 1996. *Takanobu Okamura*

stretched. The Model 382F derivative was a limited production (two aircraft) hybrid with the L-100's 501-D22 engines and the stretched fuselage. The first L-100-20 flight was on April 19, 1968, with certification following not long afterwards. While the L-100 and L-100-20 had established the Hercules in the commercial marketplace, the definitive model was yet to come. On August 14, 1970 Lockheed flew the first L-100-30/Model 382G, a further stretched model with a 100-inch plug forward and an 80-inch extension aft. The cargo compartment's

length was now 56 feet, with 6,057 cubic feet of useable volume. This was sufficient to carry three RB.211 turbofan engines at once, allowing Saturn Airways, the first customer, to transport shipsets of engines to Lockheed's L-1011 Tristar line in California from Rolls-Royce in England. As it turned out, this configuration also matched the needs of other customers, and the L-100-30 became the standard model. Again, earlier -10/20 models were also upgraded to this standard. The first flight by a -30 model took place on August 14, 1970 and within

L-100-30 PK-PLV in flight. The commercial Hercules lacks the lower cockpit windows of the military version, but nonetheless has often been used by smaller air forces. *LMASC*

several months the type had been certified and was beginning to enter service. Aside from the extended fuselage, the -30s were different in other ways as well; deleted were the JATO doors and the paratroop door windows, these being of little use for civilian operators. Among the more notable domestic L-100 operators was Southern Air Transport, which was formerly associated with the CIA's private network of airlines. The company was later sold into private hands, but would continue to carry out support and logistical flights under contract for the US, and Southern Herks were common visitors to military airfields. SAT was introduced to the Hercules in 1968-69, when it took delivery of three L-100-20 models. One of these was later rebuilt to L-100-30 configuration, and by the early 1990s more than a dozen additional stretched models had seen service with SAT, making the company the largest US operator of L-100s. Southern was also active in humanitarian operations, especially into Africa. SAT lost several Herks over the years, the first being L-100-30 N15ST, lost on takeoff at Kelly AFB, Texas on October 4, 1986. On April 8th of the following year, L-100-30 N517SJ was destroyed in a fatal crash at Travis AFB, California. Subsequently, N911SJ was written off in 1990 and the next year, N521SJ was destroyed on the ground in Sudan after hitting a mine. Despite the long history of SAT L-100 operations, that era came to an end in the summer of 1998 when Southern was acquired by Fine Air, which announced plans to consolidate SAT's fleet by selling off the Herks and other aircraft. Despite having been built for commercial use, L-100s have seen their share of use in military and paramilitary roles, with several being lost to hostile action, especially during operations in Angola, where both the government and US-backed UNITA rebels relied on the Hercules. Angolan aircraft lost in the civil war include L-100-20 D2-EAS and L-100-30s D2-THB and D2-THC. Other operators also had aircraft destroyed and crews lost, including Tepper Aviation's L-100-20 N920ST on November 27, 1989 while on a UNITA support flight. In many cases, the line between civilian and military Herks is blurred at best, especially with smaller C-130/L-100 operators. For example, military aircraft often carry out commercial operations for part of the year, sometimes operating in the colors of national airlines. Civilian Herks have also supplemented military types, such as those flown by South Africa's Safair. Air Forces that have operated L-100s include Argentina, Bolivia, Ecuador, Gabon, Kuwait, Libya, Pakistan, Peru, the Phillipines, and the United Arab Emirates. Canada has also recently taken charge of a pair of CC-130H-30s rebuilt from new L-100-30s with military systems added. Commercial Herks have moved a dizzying variety of cargo to and from all corners of the world. The original L-100-30 mission of supporting the L-1011 production line has long since ceased, but Herks continue to move large turbofan engines for airlines as needed. Another role has been support of oil drilling operations in Asia, South America, Africa, Alaska, and Canada, taking pipeline sections and drilling equipment into primitive airstrips. Other cargoes have included an orca whale ("Keiko" of "Free Willy" fame) mail, vehicles, construction equipment, airborne sprayers, and oil-spill cleanup equipment. There have been a few L-100-30 models produced for special tasks. Saudi Arabia has a half-dozen models equipped as medical aircraft, supplementing three C-130Hs configured as Air Emergency Hospitals. These have been used to provide medical care and/or medevac services to citizens throughout the Saudi kingdom, with some aircraft being fitted as mobile operating theaters, equipped with underwing electrical generating pods for self-sufficient operations in remote areas. The Saudis also operate a VIP transport model alongside military VC-130H models. Troop transport was one of the missions that the Hercules was created for, but civilian Herks have also seen some use in transporting passengers as well as cargo. Obviously, paying customers would not put up with the seating configuration used on military models, and thus pallet-mounted seats and support equipment are often used, allowing the aircraft to be rapidly turned back into a freighter. Merpati of Indonesia was the first to operate a permanently-modified Herk, this being a -30 model with 97 seats and cabin windows. Lockheed also offered a similiar new-build model with nine additional seats. Although sales of the L-100 by the mid-1990s had amounted to just over 100 aircraft, far fewer than the military C-130, Lockheed Martin still considers the commercial market a priority and is pushing the L-100J/Model 382J as the successor to the L-100-30, although by mid-1998 no orders had yet been announced.

Saudi Arabian L-100-30HS hospital ship, with underwing electrical generating pods for the onboard surgical and diagnostic equipment. *Sherman R. Pyle*

L-100-20 High Technology Test Bed

Although the C-130J did not enter service until the late 1990s, planning for a next-generation Hercules had been underway since the mid-1980s, and Lockheed's L-100-20 High Technology Test Bed program was a major part of this effort. Origi-

L-100-30 324 of the Kuwaiti Air Force, during a trip to England. *Nick Challoner*

nally a standard L-100-20 (K) of the Kuwaiti Air Force, the HTTB was bought back by Lockheed in 198_ and given the US civil registration N130X to serve as a test ship for all manner of new technologies, with an emphasis on increasing the Herk's already impressive short-field capabilities. Modifications included the fitting of horizontal and dorsal tail extensions, long-chord rudder and modified ailerons and flaps. The HTTB went on in 1985 to set new STOL records in the short takeoff and climb to three thousand, six thousand, and nine thousand-meter classes. By the late 1980s, the HTTB had once again been refitted, with the engines being replaced by T56 Series IV units each rated at 5,250 hp. Besides the extra power, these engines also operated at higher temperatures, thereby reducing smoke emissions. Thus equipped, the HTTB unofficially set a STOL weight to altitude record, as well as bettering its own climb records during tests on May 18-19, 1989 at Palmdale, California. As part of the effort to reduce the C-130's landing footprint, other alterations were also made. These included stronger landing gear for heavyweight no-flare touchdowns, a digital flight control system, and heads-up displays for the pilot and copilot, capable of being interfaced with infrared and other sensors for conducting steep approaches without outside guidance. The HTTB program came to a tragic end on February 3, 1992 when the aircraft crashed at Dobbins after becoming airborne during a high-speed taxi test of power-by-wire rudder controls, killing the entire crew.

APPENDIX A:
US C-130 Operators

USAF Hercules Units

Air Combat Command
14th Weapons Squadron/57th Wing AC-130/MC-130J
29th Weapons Squadron/USAF Weapons School. C-130J
41st Electronic Combat Squadron/55th Electronic Combat Group EC-130H
42nd Electronic Combat Squadron/55th Electronic Combat Group. TC-130H
43rd Electronic Combat Squadron/55th Electronic Combat Group EC-130H
71st Rescue Squadron/347th Rescue Group. HC-130J
79th Rescue Squadron/563rd Rescue Group HC-130J
(The 79th received it's first HC-130J, 09-5707, in November 2012)

Air Mobility Command
39th Airlift Squadron/317th Airlift Group C-130J-30
40th Airlift Squadron/317th Airlift Group C-130J-30
41st Airlift Squadron/19th Airlift Wing C-130J
53rd Airlift Squadron/19th Airlift Wing C-130H
61st Airlift Squadron/19th Airlift Wing C-130J-30
327th Airlift Squadron/913th Airlift Group C-130H

Pacific Air Forces
36th Airlift Squadron/374th Airlift Wing . . . . C-130H, to C-130J

United States Air Forces in Europe
37th Airlift Squadron/86th Airlift Wing C-130J-30

Special Operations Command
1st Special Operations Squadron/353rd SOG. MC-130H
4th Special Operations Squadron/1st SOW AC-130U
9th Special Operations Squadron/27th SOW MC-130J
15th Special Operations Squadron/1st SOW MC-130H
16th Special Operations Squadron/27th SOW AC-130J/AC-130W
17th Special Operations Squadron/353rd SOW MC-130J
19th Special Operations Squadron/1st SOG. MC-130H, AC-130U
67th Special Operations Squadron/352nd SOW. MC-130J
(The 67th retired the unit's last MC-130P, 66-0215, in February 2014)
193rd Special Operations Squadron EC-130J
415th Special Operations Squadron/58th OG. HC-130J, MC-130J
550th Special Operations Squadron/58th SOW HC-130H/P/N, MC-130H, MC-130P
551st Special Operations Squadron/AFSOAWC AC-130W, MC-130J

Air National Guard
30th Airlift Squadron/153rd Airlift Wing C-130H-3
102nd Rescue Squadron/102nd Rescue Wing HC-130N/P
109th Airlift Squadron/133rd Airlift Wing C-130H-3
115th Airlift Squadron/146th Airlift Wing C-130J-30
118th Airlift Squadron/103rd Airlift Wing C-130H

130th Airlift Squadron/130th Airlift Wing C-130H-2/3
130th Rescue Squadron/129th Rescue Wing MC-130P
139th Airlift Squadron/109th Airlift Wing LC-130H, C-130H
142nd Airlift Squadron/166th Airlift Wing. C-130H
143rd Airlift Squadron/143rd Airlift Wing C-130J-30
144th Airlift Squadron/176th Wing C-130H-2
156th Airlift Squadron/145th Airlift Wing C-130H-3
158th Airlift Squadron/165th Airlift Wing C-130H-2/3
164th Airlift Squadron/179th Airlift Wing C-130H-2
165th Airlift Squadron/123rd Airlift Wing C-130H
169th Airlift Squadron/182nd Airlift Wing. C-130H-3
180th Airlift Squadron/139th Airlift Wing C-130H-2/2.5
181st Airlift Squadron/136th Airlift Wing C-130H
186th Airlift Squadron/120th Airlift Wing C-130H
187th Airlift Squadron/153rd Airlift Wing C-130H-3
192nd Airlift Squadron/152 Airlift Wing C-130H
198th Airlift Squadron/156 Airlift Wing. C-130H
211th Rescue Squadron/176th Wing. HC-130N

Air Force Reserve Command
5th Special Operations Squadron/919th SOW AC-130U
39th Rescue Squadron/920th Rescue Wing HC-130P
53rd Weather Reconnaissance Squadron/403rd Wing . . . WC-130J
95th Airlift Squadron/440th AW. C-130H-2
96th Airlift Squadron/934th Airlift Wing C-130H-3
328th Airlift Squadron/914th Airlift Wing C-130H-2
357th Airlift Squadron/908th Airlift Wing C-130H-2
700th Airlift Squadron/94th Airlift Wing C-130H-3
731st Airlift Squadron/302nd Airlift Wing. C-130H-3
757th Airlift Squadron/910th Airlift Wing C-130H-2
758th Airlift Squadron/911th Airlift Wing C-130H-2
815th Airlift Squadron/403rd Wing C-130J

Air Force Materiel Command
413th Flight Test Squadron/96th Test Wing HC-130J, MC-130J, AC-130J
418th Flight Test Squadron/412th Test Wing C-130J

Air Education Training Command
48th Airlift Squadron/314th Airlift Wing C-130J

USN/USMC Hercules Units
VR-53 . . . . C-130T Andrews AFB
VR-54 . . . . C-130T NAS New Orleans
VR-55 . . . . C-130T NAS Point Mugu
VR-62 . . . . C-130T NAS Jacksonville
VR-64 . . . . C-130T McGuire AFB

Navy Flight Demonstration Squadron Blue Angels C-130T

VX-1	KC-130J	NAS Patuxent River
VX-20		NAS Patuxent River
VX-30		NAS Point Mugu
VX-31		NAWS China Lake

VMGR-152	KC-130J	MCAS Futenma, Japan
VMGR-234	KC-130J	NASJRB Fort Worth
VMGR-252	KC-130J	MCAS Cherry point
VMGR-352	KC-130J	MCAS Miramar
VMGR-452	KC-130J	Stewart ANGB

USAF C-130 Serial Numbers

C-130A
53-3129/3135
54-1621/1640
55-0001/0048
56-0468/0551
57-0453/0483

Test Aircraft:
Converted to AC-130A:

Converted to C-130A-II: 54-1637, 56-0484, 56-0525, 56-0530, 56-0534, 56-0535, 56-0537, 56-0538, 56-0540, 56-0541

Converted to RC-130S: 56-0493

Converted to WC-130A: 56-0519, 56-0522, 56-0537

Attrition: 55-0038, 55-0039, 55-0042, 55-0043, 56-0472, 56-0477, 56-0480, 56-0488, 56-0499, 56-0502, 56-0506, 56-0510, 56-0515, 56-0516, 56-0526, 56-0528, 56-0533, 56-0548, 56-0549, 57-0454, 57-0467, 57-0468, 57-0475

Stored at AMARC 1997: 53-3134, 55-0004, 55-0024, 55-0026, 55-0033, 55-0036, 55-0041, 56-0470, 56-0471, 56-0481, 56-0484, 56-0485, 56-0486, 56-0494, 56-0503, 56-0523, 56-0529, 56-0543, 56-0544, 57-0458, 57-0456, 57-0463

Air Tankers: 54-1631 (N117TG, Tanker 31, T&G Aviation), 56-0473 (N473TM, Tanker 63, TBM Inc.), 56-0478 (N116TG, Tanker 30 T&G Aviation, lost in France 200), 56-0511 (N132FF, Tanker 83, HVFS), 56-0530 (N131FF, Tanker 81, HVFS), 56-0531 (N531BA, Tanker 67, TBM Inc.), 57-0466 (N466TM, Tanker 64, TBM, Inc.)

C-130D
57-0484/0495

Attrition:

Stored at AMARC 1997: 57-0488, 57-0492, 57-0494

RC-130A
57-0510/0524

Air Tankers: 57-0512 (N118TG, T&G Aviation), 57-0520 (N138FF, Tanker 88, HVFS)

C-130B

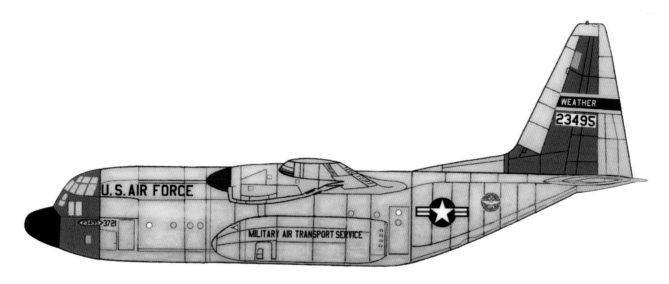

WC-130B 62-3495. After being used for atmospheric sampling missions this aircraft was reconfigured as a transport and later transferred to Tunisia. *Chris Reed*

57-0525/0529
58-0711/0758
59-1524/1537
59-5957
60-0293/0310
60-5450/5453 (For Canada)
61-0948/0972
61-2634/2649
62-4140/4143 (For Pakistan)

Converted to C-130B-II: 58-0711, 59-1524, 59-1525, 59-1526, 59-1527, 59-1528, 59-1530, 59-1531, 59-1532, 59-1533, 59-1535, 59-1537

Converted to JC-130B: 61-0962/0963

Converted to WC-130B: 58-0725, 58-0726, 58-0729, 58-0731, 58-0733, 58-0734, 58-0740

Test Aircraft: 57-0526, 57-0527, 57-0528, 57-0529, 58-0712, 58-0713, 58-0714, 58-0716, 58-0717, 58-0750

Transferred to Argentina: 61-0964, 61-0969

Transferred to Bolivia: 61-0968

Transferred to Columbia: 58-0726 (ex-WC), 61-0956, 61-2639

Transferred to Ecuador: 58-0733 (ex-WC)

Transferred to Greece: 61-0948

Transferred to Indonesia: 58-0748, 60-0305, 60-0306, 60-0309

Transferred to Iran: 62-3488/3491 (Later transferred to Pakistan)

Transferred to Pakistan: 61-2646, 61-2648

Transferred to the Philippines: 58-0725 (ex-WC)

Transferred to Romania: 61-0950

Transferred to Singapore: 58-0724, 58-0756

Transferred to Tunisia: 61-0949

Transferred to Turkey: 61-0960, 61-0963, 61-2634

Transferred to Uruguay: 60-0295, 61-0971

Attrition: 58-0718, 58-0719, 58-0721, 58-0722, 58-0730, 58-0737, 58-0743, 58-0745, 59-1534, 60-0293, 60-0297, 60-0298, 60-0307, 60-0475, 61-0815, 61-0953, 61-0955, 61-0965, 61-0967, 61-0970, 61-0972, 61-2637, 61-2641, 61-2642, 61-2644, 61-2648, 61-2649

Stored at AMARC 1997: 58-0713, 58-0714, 58-0715, 58-0729, 58-0734, 58-0742, 58-0750, 58-0754, 58-0757, 59-1525, 59-1529, 59-1536, 59-1537, 61-0958, 61-0959, 61-0962, 61-2643, 62-3495

C-130E (Lockheed Martin Model 382-4B/8B/13B/16B)
61-2358/2373
62-1784/1866
63-7764/7899
63-9810/9817
63-13186/13189 (For Turkey)
64-0495/0572
64-17624/17639 (For Canada)
64-17680/17681
64-18240
65-10686/10689 (For Iran)
65-12766/12769 (For Canada)
65-12896/12907 (For Australia)
66-4310/4313 (For Iran)
67-14726/14729 (For Iran)
68-10934/10951
69-6566/6583
69-7706/7710 (For Iran)
70-1259/1276
71-0213/0223 (For Iran)
72-01288/01299

Converted to AC-130E: 69-6567, 69-6568, 69-6569, 69-6570, 69-6571 (w/o) 69-6572, 69-6573, 69-6574, 69-6574, 69-6575, 69-6576, 69-6577

Converted to C-130E-II: 62-1819, 62-1822, 62-1828

Converted to DC-130E: 61-2361, 61-2362, 61-2363, 61-2364, 61-2368, 61-2369, 61-2371

Converted to ABCCC: 62-1791, 62-1809, 62-1818, 62-1825, 62-1832, 62-1836, 62-1857, 62-1863

Converted to EC-130E(RR): 63-7773, 63-7783, 63-7815, 63-7816, 63-7828, 63-7869, 63-9816, 63-9817

Converted to MC-130E: 63-7785, 64-0523, 64-0523, 64-0547, 64-0551, 64-0555, 64-0558, 64-0559, 64-0561, 64-0562, 64-0563, 64-0564, 64-0565, 64-0566, 64-0567, 64-0568, 64-0571, 64-0572

64-0567 has been on display at Hurlburt Field since 2011

Converted to WC-130E: 61-2360, 61-2365, 61-2366, 64-0532, 64-0553, 64-0554

Transferred to Israel: 63-7774, 63-7810, 63-7843, 63-7844, 63-7855, 63-7862, 63-7870, 64-0509, 64-0516, 64-0528

Attrition: 62-1785, 62-1797, 62-1800, 62-1802, 62-1805, 62-1813, 62-1814, 62-1815, 62-1831, 62-1840, 62-1841, 62-1845, 62-1853, 62-1854, 62-1861, 62-1865, 63-7772, 63-7780, 63-7785, 63-7798, 63-7827, 63-7854, 63-7875, 64-0508, 64-0511

Stored at AMARC 1997: 61-2360, 61-2365, 62-1803, 62-1865, 63-7771, 63-7803, 63-7806, 63-7836, 64-0497, 64-0503, 64-0513, 64-0530, 64-0552

C-130E 62-1863, having been converted to HC-130P standard, was retired in March 2015, at which time it was the USAF's oldest active C-130.

HC-130H
64-14852/14866
65-0962/0987
65-0989/0990

Converted to DC-130H: 65-0971, 65-0974, 65-0979

Converted to JC-130H: 64-14854, 64-14857, 64-14858

Converted to WC-130H: 64-14861, 65-0963, 65-0964, 65-0965, 65-0966, 65-0967, 65-0968, 65-0969, 65-0972, 65-0976, 65-0977, 65-0984, 65-0985

Converted to tankers: 64-14858 (MC), 64-14860 (HC), 64-14863 (HC), 64-14864 (HC), 64-14865 (HC), 65-0970 (HC), 65-0971 (MC), 65- 0973 (HC), 65-0974 (HC), 65-0975 (MC), 65-0978 (HC), 65-0981 (HC), 65-0982 (HC), 65-0983 (HC), 65-0986 (HC), 65-0988 (HC), 65-0991 (MC), 65-0992 (MC), 65-0993 (MC), 65-0994 (MC)

Attrition: 65-0990

HC-130P
65-0988
65-0991/0994
66-0211/0225

Converted to MC-130P: 66-0212, 66-0213, 66-0215, 66-0216, 66-0217, 66-0219, 66-0220, 66-0223, 66-0225

Attrition: 66-0214, 66-0213, 66-0218

MC-130P 66-0213 was the first US Herk lost during the War on Terror, crashing in Afghanistan on February 13, 2002.

HC-130N
69-5819/5833

C-130H
64-15094/15096 (For New Zealand)
68-8218/8219 (For New Zealand)
68-10952/10957 (For Norway)
71-1067/1069 (For Zaire)
71-1374/1375 (For Israel)
75-0534/0539 (For Israel)
75-0542/0549 (For Greece)
76-1598/1603 (For Egypt)
77-1741/1742 (For Portugal)
78-0726 (For Portugal)
78-0745/0750 (For Sudan)
78-0806/0813
79-0473/0480
79-1714/1716 (For Thailand)
80-0320/0326
80-0332
81-0001 (For Oman)
81-0626/0631
82-0050 (For Oman)
82-0051/0052 (For Japan)
82-0054/0061
82-0086/0088 (For Egypt)
82-0666 (For Thailand)
83-0001/0002 (For Japan)
83-0486/0489
84-0204/0213
85-0035/0042
85-1361/1368
86-0372/0373 (For Japan)
86-0410/0415
86-0418/0419
86-1391/1398
87-0137/0138 (For Japan)
87-9281/9288
88-1301/1308
88-1800/1802 (For Japan)
88-4401/4408
89-0118/0119 (For Japan)
89-1051/1056
89-1181/1188
89-9101/9106
90-1057/1058
90-1791/1798
90-9107/9108
91-1231/1239
91-1651/1653

91-9141/9144
92-0547/0554
92-1451/1454
92-1531/1538
92-3021/3024
92-3281/3288
93-1036/1041
93-1455/1459
93-1561/1563
93-2041/2042
93-7311/7314
94-3026/3027
94-6702/6708
94-7310/7321
95-6709/6712
96-1001/1008
96-7332/7325

Transferred to Canada: 73-1589, 73-1591 73-1593, 73-1596, 73-1599

MC-130W Conversions: 87-9286, 88-1301/1308

The increased need for special operations forces post 9-11, coupled with the loss of several MC-130s, led to a program to refit C-130H-2 airframes to a special ops configuration. Although the resulting MC-130Ws (officially named Combat Spear in 2007) lack the terrain following/avoidance capability of the Combat Talons, they are fitted out with counterneasures, secure communications, and provisions for refueling helicopters. The MC-130Ws have been further retrofitted as interim gunships, with a GAU-23/A Bushmaster 30 mm cannon, GBU-39 Small Diameter Bomb, and AGM-176 Griffon capability. Originally dubbed Dragon Spear, these aircraft were redesignated AC-130W Stinger IIs in May 2012.

AC-130U conversions: 87-0128, 89-0509/0514, 89-1051/1056, 90-0163/0167, 92-0253

Supplemental conversions: in the last days of 2001, with the US facing an open-ended counterterrorism commitment, the Air Force was directed to purchase an additional four AC-130Us; as the baseline C-130H airframe was out of production, this meant existing aircraft would have to be converted, with extra C-130Js being bought to replace them in the transport role. Although the "Plus 4" AC-130Us were intended to be minimal change aircraft to speed their conversions, they initially had one major armament change: the removal of the aging 40 mm Bofors and the hard-to-support GAU-12/Us, and the fitting of a pair of 30 mm Mk 44 Mod 0 Bushmaster cannon in return. It was intended to refit this weapon to existing AC-130Us as well, but testing showed the Bushmaster suffered accuracy problems at the AC-130U's typical operating altitude, so the 30 mm guns were taken off and the Bofors were installed.

LC-130H (Lockheed Martin Model 382C-47E)
83-0490/0493

MC-130H
84-0475/0476
85-0011/0022
87-0023/0024
87-0125/0127
88-0191/0195
88-0264
88-1803

89-0280/0283
90-0161/0162

To date, two MC-130Hs have been lost in the War on Terror: 84-0875 in Afghanistan during July 2002, and 85-0012 in Iraq in December 2004. Additionally, 90-0161 was lost in a crash in Puerto Rico, while 87-0127 went down in Albania.

C-130J
97-5303/5306

C-130J-30
99-1431/1433
02-1434, 02-1463/1464
03-3142/3144
04-8153
05-1435/1436, 05-1465/1466, 05-3145/3147
06-1437/1438, 06-1467, 06-4631/4634, 06-8159, 06-8610/8612
07-1468, 07-4631/4639, 07-8608/8609, 07-8613/8614
08-3172/3179, 08-5675

HC-130J
09-0108/0109, 09-5706/5709
10-5716/5717
11-5719, 11-5725, 11-5727
12-5755, 12-5765, 12-5768

MC-130J
08-5697, 08-6201/6206,
09-5710/5711, 09-5713, 09-6207/6210
10-5714,
11-5729, 11-5731/5733, 11-5735,11-5737, 12-5757
12-5759/5760
13-5772, 13-5777/5779
14-5791, 14-5796, 14-5800, 14-5802, 14-5805, 14-5808/5809
(MC-130J 11-5737 was the 300th C-130J model delivered)

WC-130J
96-5300/5302

USN/USMC Hercules Bureau Numbers

C-130F (GV-1U)
149787
149790
149793-149794
149797
149801
149805

Transferred to South Africa: 149783, 149787

LC-130F (C-130BL)

148318/148320

Attrition: 148320

KC-130F (GV-1)
149788/149789
149791/149792
149795/149796
149798/149800
149802/149804
149806/149816

Attrition: 149802, 149809, 149810, 149813, 149814, 150685

EC-130G (C-130G)
151888/151891

Converted to TC-130G: 151888, 151891

EC-130Q
156170/156177
159348
159469
160608
161223
161328
161494/161496
161531
162312/162313

Converted to TC-130Q: 159348, 159469

Attrition: 156176

160608 to N14781, to Klu as C-130H
161495 to N130FF/Tanker 131
161531 to N41RF
162313 to N9239G, to Klu as C-130H

LC-130R
155919
159129/159133
160740/160741

C-130T
164762/164763
164993/164998
165158/165161
165313/165314
165348/165351
165378/165379

KC-130T
162308/162311
162785/162786
163022/163023
163310/163311
163591/163592
164105/164106
164180/164181
164194/164195
164441/164442
164597/164598
164759/164760
164999/165000
165162/165163
165315/165316
165352/165353

Coast Guard C-130s

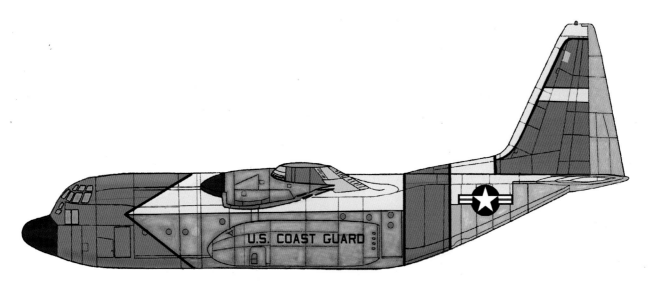

R8V-1G (SC-130B) 1342 of the US Coast Guard as delivered, before being numbered. *Chris Reed*

USCG Serial Type USAF Identity
1344/1345 SC/HC-130B 60-0311/0312
1349 SC/HC-130B 62-3753
1351 SC/HC-130B 62-3754
1356 SC/HC-130B 62-3755
1414 EC-130E 66-4299
1452/1454 HC-130E 67-7183/7185
1500/1502 HC-130H 72-1300/1301
1503/1504 HC-130H 73-0844/0845
1600/1603 HC-130H 77-0317/0320
1700/1704 HC-130H-7 82-0081/0085

1705 HC-130H 83-0007
1706/1709 HC-130H-7 83-0505/0508
1710/1713 HC-130H 84-0479/0482
1714/1715 HC-130H 85-0051/0052
1716 HC-130H 85-1360
1717/1719 HC-130H 86-0420/0422
1790 HC-130H-7 81-0999

USAF Hercules Units

Air Combat Command
41st ECCS EC-130H
42nd ECCS TC-130H
43rd ECCS EC-130H
71st Rescue Squadron HC-130P, HC-130J
79th Rescue Squadron HC-130J
(The 79th received its first HC-130J, 09-5707, in November 2012)
211th Rescue Squadron HC-130N

Air Mobility Command
39th Airlift Squadron C-130J-30
40th Airlift Squadron C-130J-30
41st Airlift Squadron C-130H-30
53rd Airlift Squadron C-130H
61st Airlift Squadron C-130J-30
327th Airlift Squadron C-130H
357th Airlift Squadron C-130H-2
815th Airlift Squadron C-130J/J-30

Pacific Air Forces
36th Airlift Squadron C-130H

United States Air Forces in Europe
37th Airlift Squadron C-130J-30

Special Operations Command
1st Special Operations Squadron MC-130H
4th Special Operations Squadron AC-130U
9th Special Operations Squadron MC-130J
15th Special Operations Squadron MC-130H
16th Special Operations Squadron AC-130J/AC-130W
17th Special Operations Squadron MC-130J
67th Special Operations Squadron MC-130J
(The 67th retired the unit's last MC-130P, 66-0215, in February 2014)
193rd Special Operations Squadron EC-130J
550th Special Operations Squadron HC-130H/P/N, MC-130H, MC-130P

Air National Guard
30th Airlift Squadron C-130H-3
102nd Rescue Squadron HC-130N/P
109th Airlift Squadron C-130H
115th Airlift Squadron C-130J-30
118th Airlift Squadron C-130H

130th Airlift Squadron C-130H-3
130th Rescue Squadron MC-130P
139th Airlift Squadron LC-130H, C-130H
142nd Airlift Squadron C-130H
143rd Airlift Squadron C-130J-30
156th Airlift Squadron C-130H-3
158th Airlift Squadron C-130H
164th Airlift Squadron C-130H
165th Airlift Squadron C-130H
169th Airlift Squadron C-130H-2/H-3
180th Airlift Squadron C-130H
181st Airlift Squadron C-130H
186th Airlift Squadron C-130H
192nd Airlift Squadron C-130H
198th Airlift Squadron WC-130H

Air Force Reserve Command
39th Rescue Squadron HC-130N/P
53rd Weather Reconnaissance Squadron WC-130J
95th Airlift Squadron C-130H
96th Airlift Squadron C-130H-3
328th Airlift Squadron C-130H
700th Airlift Squadron C-130H
757th Airlift Squadron C-130H-2
758th Airlift Squadron C-130H-2

APPENDIX C:
Overseas Hercules Operators

Afghanistan: Four C-130H. The first two aircraft were turned over in October 2013.

Algeria: Fifteen C-130H

Argentina: 1 KC-130H, four C-130, L-100

Australia: Twelve C-130J-30. The J models replaced the RAAF's C-130Es and the C-130Hs were retired in late 2012, with most being passed on to Indonesia.

Bangladesh: Four C-130B, four C-130Es requested.

Belgium: Ten C-130H of 12 delivered

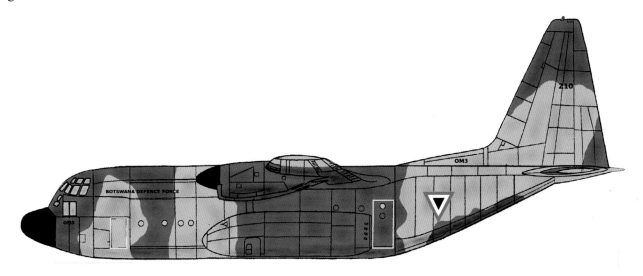

Botswana Defense Force C-130B OM3, formerly USAF 58-0742, transferred in 2000 after storage at AMARC. *Chris Reed*

Bolivia: Three C-130B

Botswana: Three C-130B

Brazil: 15x C-130E/H/M, 2x KC-130. C-130M FAB2470 seriously damaged in November 2014 at King George Island, Antarctica.

Cameroon: Three C-130H

Canada: 17x CC-130J-30; receipt of these aircraft allowed the phaseout of the twenty surviving CC-130Es by 2012. Surviving CC-130H/H-30/H(T) remain in service.

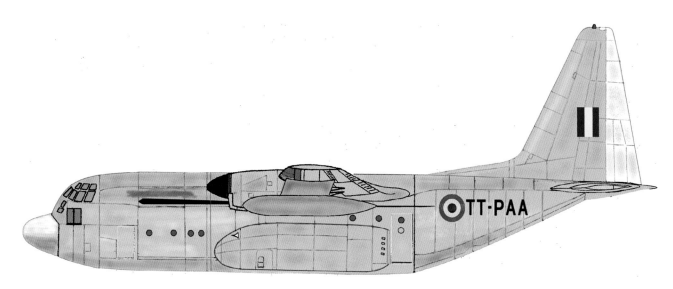

C-130A TT-PAA of the Chad Air Force, displaying the remnants of the markings it wore as RAAF A97-208, having been supplied via France. It was later broken up. *Chris Reed*

Chad: One C-130H, 1 aircraft lost in 2006

Chile: Three C-130B/H, two KC-130R on order

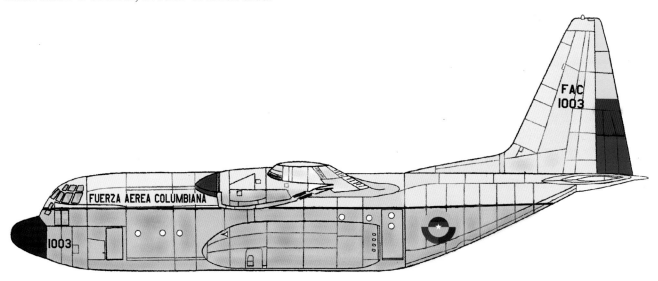

Having started out life as RCAF 10301, C-130B 1003 of the Fuerza Aérea Colombiana was lost after ditching in the Atlantic in 1982. *Chris Reed*

Columbia: Seven C-130B/H

Denmark: Four C-130J-30

Ecuador: Four C-130E/H; C-130Bs retired.

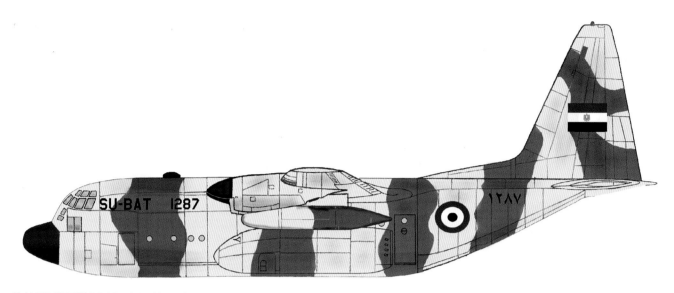

C-130H 1287/SU-BAT of the Egyptian Air Force. *Chris Reed*

Egypt: 22x C-130H, 2x C-130H-30, 2x EC-130H

Ethiopia: Two C-130B/E

France: 7x C-130H, 7x C-130H-30. In November 2015, France requested two transport model C-130Js and a pair of KC-130J tankers to fill a gap in tactical transport capability as the C.160 force aged and problems delayed the A400M.

Greece: Twelve C-130H, 3-5 C-130B

Honduras: One C-130A

India: Five C-130J-30SH, with 6+ on order. The first Indian aircraft, KC3801, flew on October 4, 2012. The Indian J models are notable in that they are equipped with the AN/AAQ-32 EO/IR sensor system.

Indonesia: One KC-130B, 13 C-130B/H, 4 L-100

Iran: Nineteen C-130E/H

Iraq: Two C-130E, three C-130J-30. The first Iraqi J model was delivered in December 2012.

Israel: Six C-130E, six C-130H. Nine C-130J-30 Shimshon (Samson) in service/on order, with the first being turned over in April 2014.

Italy: Eleven C-130J, ten C-130J-30. C-130Hs retired 2001

Japan: Fifteen C-130H. Six KC-130Rs in storage at AMARC have been bought to receive structural refits and glass cockpits

Jordan: Seven C-130E/H; three ex-USAF C-130Es were transferred in 2011–2012

Malaysia: Ten C-130H, 1 C-130MP, four KC-130T

Mexico: Seven C-130E, C-130K, L-100

Netherlands: Two C-130H-30, two EC-130Q converted to C-130H standard

New Zealand: Five C-130H

Norway: Four C-130J-30 + 1 replacement for a lost aircraft. Formerly six C-130H

Oman: Three C-130H, one C-130J-30 +2

Pakistan: Five C-130B, eleven C-130E

Peru: L-100-20

Philippines: One C-130B + more stored, two C-130H, + two C-130T on order

Poland: Five C-130E. The first Polish Hercules was delivered in March 2009

Portugal: Five C-130H

Qatar: Four C-130J-30. The first Qatari Super Hercules flew in June 2011.

Romania: C-130B/H. H model is ex-Italy.

Saudia Arabia: Thirty C-130E/H, seven KC-130H, five VC-130H, twenty C-130J-30 on order, five KC-130J-30 on order

Singapore: Two C-130B, two KC-130B, five C-130H, one KC-130H

South Korea: C-130H, C-130H-30, four C-130J. The first RoKAF J model was rolled out from Marietta in Njune 2013, with handover of the first two aircraft taking place in March the following year.

Sri Lanka: C-130K

Sudan: Four C-130H

Sweden: Survivors from eight C-130E/Tp 84 brought up to C-130H standard

Taiwan: 1 C-130HE EW, nineteen C-130H

Tunisia: Two C-130J. Tunisia was the first African customer for the J model, supplementing seven C-130Bs and a solitary C-130H.

UAE: One C-130H-30, three C-130H, three L-100-30. Requirement for 12 C-130J-30s.

Uruguay: Two C-130B

Venezuela: Four C-130H